Trees and Their Environment

A Collection of CEU Articles

This compendium is worth a total of 8.5 CEU credits.

International Society of Arboriculture®

The ISA seal is a registered trademark.

International Society of Arboriculture
P.O. Box 3129
Champaign, IL 61826-3129
www.isa-arbor.com
isa@isa-arbor.com

10 9 8 7 6 5
ISBN 1-881956-37-7
04-08/RF/500

Acknowledgments

ISA wishes to thank the following people for their contributions to this publication:

Technical Review: Todd Watson, Texas A&M University

Technical Review and Project Development: Sharon Lilly, ISA

Reviewer: Ramon Johnston, ISA arborist intern

Editorial and Production Manager: Peggy Currid, ISA

Editorial and Production Support: Kathy Ashmore, ISA; Joan Wagner, ISA editorial intern

Cover Art: Bryan Kotwica

Design and Layout: Amy Reiss

Proofreaders: Phyl Good and Erin Cler

Table of Contents

Introduction

The scientist B.F. Skinner once said, "Education is what survives when what has been learned has been forgotten."

Whether you are in search of a review of concepts you learned in previous CEU articles or are looking to strengthen your knowledge of arboriculture by reading these collected articles for the first time, the CEU compendium you hold in your hands is designed to further your arboriculture education.

Each compendium is a compilation of previously published CEU articles from 1993 to the present. The articles have been sorted into seven different major categories and can be purchased separately or as a set. The seven categories are

Tree Biology

Plant Health Care

Safe Work Practices

Tree Maintenance

Trees and Their Environment

Tree Selection and Planting

Tree Diagnosis and Treatment

The compendia's primary purpose is continuing education. Many of these CEU articles address issues arborists deal with on a daily basis, and they serve as an invaluable resource for arborists around the world. The diversity of topics will help you expand your knowledge and give you a better understanding of tree health and maintenance. The compendia also can serve as a good teaching tool for business owners or arboriculture teachers to expand the knowledge base of their employees or students.

If you are an ISA Certified Arborist or Certified Tree Worker, you are required to earn continuing education credits to sustain your certification. With work, family, and other responsibilities, it can sometimes be difficult to squeeze seminars or courses into your schedule. The compendia provide you with the opportunity to meet these requirements on your own time. And in the compendia, these CEU articles are now available to members and Certified Arborists who became involved in ISA after the original publication dates.

Even if you've already read the article and earned CEU credits on it, you can still review the article and submit answers for credit once again. Questions have been revamped from their original publication so that members can "retake" each article's quiz. However, submitting quiz answers from the compendia will be the last opportunity to earn CEU credits on these articles.

When submitting answers for CEU questions, you must answer on the official sheets enclosed in the book. No photocopies or substitutions will be accepted.

Although school might have been completed long ago, arboriculture is a constantly evolving profession that requires you to also be a student of nature. Remember: The day you stop learning is the day your professionalism dies.

Back to Basics: Tree Fertilization

By Bruce W. Hagen

Urban soils and the natural processes that sustain them are strongly affected by development and human activities. Soil structure, which influences aeration, drainage, and water-holding capacity, is most notably affected. Organic matter content, pH, mineral availability, and other characteristics can be unfavorably altered by construction-related activities and by various horticultural practices.

These impacts can adversely affect tree growth, vitality, longevity, and appearance. For instance, topsoil is removed routinely during construction, and the subsoil becomes severely compacted. Often the result is a hard, nearly impenetrable, poorly aerated, nutrient-poor root environment with reduced water-holding capacity. Water penetration and soil aeration are further restricted by pavement, which is often placed around trees and limits the volume of soil favorable for root growth. Leaves and other tree debris are removed regularly, disrupting nutrient cycling and the deposition of organic matter—an important component of fertile soils. Moreover, the activity of soil microorganisms that release minerals bound in organic matter, fix atmospheric nitrogen (convert it to available forms), and enhance mineral absorption is often greatly reduced.

Foliar symptoms of mineral deficiencies include chlorosis and smaller and fewer leaves, but often the first noticeable response is slow growth. What often appear as nutritional problems, though, are more likely symptoms of other environmental factors, such as soil compaction, poor aeration, dry

Learning objectives—
The arborist will be able to

- describe some of the environmental factors and human activities that affect essential mineral availability to trees.

- explain the effects of soil pH, cation exchange capacity, and textural characteristics on mineral availability and tree health.

- list the potential benefits and limitations of tree fertilization.

or saturated soil, salt damage, high or low soil pH, pest problems, air pollution, or herbicides. In most cases, soil mineral content is less important than water availability, soil texture, structure, depth, and organic matter content.

Although judicious fertilization can increase growth and help maintain tree health, it is not always necessary or beneficial. Excess fertilization can injure roots, burn foliage, increase susceptibility to certain insects, reduce tolerance to environmental stress, increase maintenance costs, and contaminate groundwater.

Fertilization can be a useful tool to promote rapid growth in nursery trees; encourage moderate growth in young, established trees; maintain health in mature trees; and correct known nutrient deficiencies. An understanding of how trees respond to changes in soil fertility and moisture availability is critical to the effective use of fertilizer and irrigation in the landscape.

The Basics

Trees do not obtain energy directly from mineral nutrients in the soil. They obtain it by converting light energy (sunlight) to chemical energy (sugar) during photosynthesis:

$$6CO_2 \text{ (carbon dioxide)} + 12H_2O \text{ (water)} + \text{chlorophyll/light} =$$
$$C_6H_{12}O_6 \text{ (glucose)} + 6O_2 \text{ (oxygen)} + 6H_2O$$

Photosynthesis is an energy-trapping process that manufactures sugars (glucose, sucrose, etc.) using energy from the sun, carbon dioxide (CO_2) from the air, and water (H_2O) from the soil. Glucose, a carbohydrate, is the starting point for all other plant-related compounds (such as cellulose, protein, and fats). During respiration, glucose is broken down to release stored energy to perform the tree's biochemical processes.

Mineral elements are the basic building blocks for new growth and cellular function. Trees require 18 essential elements for normal growth:

carbon (C)	iron (Fe)
hydrogen (H)	manganese (Mn)
oxygen (O)	boron (B)
nitrogen (N)	molybdenum (Mo)
phosphorus (P)	nickel (Ni)
potassium (K)	copper (Cu)
calcium (Ca)	zinc (Zn)
magnesium (Mg)	chlorine (Cl)
sulfur (S)	cobalt (Co)

Except for carbon (C) and oxygen (O_2), these elements and water (H_2O) are taken up by the roots. Nearly all elements are absorbed as charged particles (*ions*) in the soil water. Nutrients required in large quantities (N, P,

Fertilization: Points to Remember

- Nitrogen is a growth stimulant, promoting both root and shoot growth. It also improves leaf color by increasing the level of chlorophyll.
- Trees are adapted to low levels of nitrogen; thus, high rates are generally undesirable.
- Phosphorus, unless deficient, does not stimulate root growth as popularly believed. Neither phosphorus nor potassium stimulate growth (root, shoot) unless a deficiency in those elements exists.
- The routine use of fertilizer containing nitrogen, phosphorus, and potassium is largely unjustified unless a deficiency exists.
- Plants can't distinguish between manufactured and natural fertilizers. Natural fertilizers and those with high water-insoluble nitrogen levels release nitrogen and other nutrients slowly. Manures, however, may be high in salts. Composted (aged) manure is preferred because the nitrogen is organically bound and thus gradually released.
- Trees growing in regularly fertilized and well-irrigated turf may not require supplemental fertilization. Although the grass roots absorb much of the nitrogen, sufficient levels may reach tree roots to stimulate moderate tree growth.
- Consider an alternative to fertilization—yearly mulching of a tree's drip zone with coarse wood chips or leaves may provide adequate nutrition.

K, S, Ca, and Mg) are *macronutrients*. The others, needed in trace amounts, are *micronutrients*.

Mineral elements from organic matter decomposition, soil weathering (mineralization), fertilizer application, environmental deposition, and nitrogen fixation are dissolved in the soil water or *adsorbed* (weakly held) to charged soil particles and organic matter (*colloids*). The minerals are absorbed by the roots as ions (charged atoms or molecules). Ions carrying a plus (+) charge—for example, Ca^{++} or Mg^{++}—are called *cations*. Those with a negative (–) charge, such as NO_3^- or SO_4^{--}, are *anions*. The charge carried by each ion affects its behavior in the soil.

Cation Exchange Capacity

Cation exchange capacity (CEC) indicates the soil's ability to store cations. It is a measure of the soil's potential fertility. Cations resist leaching by water and thus remain available for absorption by tree roots. The CEC of a soil depends largely on the content of clay particles and humus (organic matter). These colloidal particles have charged and chemically active surfaces that attract ions. Negative charges generally predominate on most soil colloids. Cations, and anions to some extent, are held at the charged-ion exchange sites, where they can be exchanged by other ions. As cations or anions are absorbed from the soil by tree roots, additional ions are released from their exchange sites into the soil to maintain equilibrium. Roots also absorb ions directly from the cation exchange sites. Cation exchange capacity can be affected by soil pH. For instance, hydrogen (H^+) or aluminum (Al^{+++}), both of which are nonessential nutrients, occupy many of the cation exchange sites in acid soils. Thus, other essential cations are less available. Anions, which carry a negative charge, are less likely to be adsorbed by colloidal particles and are thus more subject to leaching. Some anions are held predominantly in the soil as complex compounds largely unavailable for plant uptake. Organic matter is an important source of anions, particularly nitrogen and phosphorus. These *bound* mineral ions are released during decomposition by microbial activity (mineralization).

Soil Reaction

Soil reaction (pH) affects the solubility of mineral nutrients and thus their availability to plants. Soil pH is a measure of the soil's acidity or alkalinity. It is determined by the concentration of hydrogen (H^+) and hydroxyl (OH^-) ions.

The following problems are associated with strongly acid (low pH) soils:

- reduced availability of cations: hydrogen (H^+) or aluminum (Al^{+++}) ions occupy many of the cation exchange sites
- increased solubility of manganese (Mn^{++}) and Al^{+++}, both of which are toxic at high levels
- reduced soil bacterial activity (nitrogen-fixing and organic matter decomposing organisms)
- H^+ ions occupy most of the cation exchange sites, favoring the loss of other cations

Adding limestone to acid soils improves fertility by substituting the cation Ca^{++} (calcium) for H^+.

$$2H^+ + CaCO_3 \rightarrow Ca^{++} + H_2O + CO_2$$

On the other hand, in alkaline soils (high pH), many nutrients (such as Zn, Fe, Mn, and P) become increasingly unavailable as pH increases. Also, alkaline soils are typically toxic, poorly aggregated, poorly drained, and difficult to wet. Lack of adequate leaching in arid and semi-arid areas leaves the soil high in cations (such as CA^{++}, Mg^+, K^+, and Na^+). Consequently, soil pH is typically greater than 7 and sometimes as high as 10. Soils high in soluble salts have a detrimental impact on plant growth. Excess salts restrict water uptake and injure root cells.

Sulfur dust or granules often are used to reduce salinity in alkaline soils. Elemental sulfur added to saline soil in the presence of water and oxygen forms sulfuric acid (H_2SO_4), which in turn reacts with lime ($CaCO_3$) to yield gypsum ($CaSO_4$):

$$CaCO_3 + H_2SO_4 \rightarrow CO_2 + CaSO_4 + H_2O$$

Thoroughly mixed gypsum added to sodic (high-sodium) soil replaces the Na^{++} held by the soil colloids with Ca^{++}:

$$CaSO_4 + NaCO_3 \rightarrow CaCO_3 + Na_2SO_4$$

This reaction forms sodium sulfate, which is readily soluble, allowing Na^+ to leach away when irrigated. Sulfuric acid also reacts directly with sodic soil to yield a soluble form of sodium while reducing alkalinity:

$$Na_2CO_3 + H_2SO_4 \rightarrow NaSO_4 + CO_2 + H_2O$$

In this reaction, Na$^+$ is replaced by H$^+$, and the carbonate ion is eliminated. If appreciable lime is present in the saline or sodic soil, sulfur or sulfuric acid may be added to form gypsum. Another method to improve drainage and gradually reduce pH is to incorporate certain organic material or mulch the soil with organic matter.

Nutrient Deficiencies

Nitrogen

Nitrogen provides the most universal response to plant growth because it is the most limiting nutrient in the soil. Optimal levels of nitrogen often do not exist because nitrogen is bound in biomass and woody debris. It leaches from the soil in the soil water and is quickly converted back to the gaseous state (a process known as *volatilization*). Soil nitrogen content, despite loss to leaching, volatilization, and denitrification by soil organisms, remains relatively constant because of natural deposition of nitrogen from the atmosphere, release of minerals bound in organic matter, and the nitrogen fixed by soil bacteria. The continual removal of natural leaf litter and the harvesting of fruits and nuts can gradually deplete soil nitrogen, however. Nitrogen also can be temporarily tied up by soil organisms during decomposition.

Although the level of nitrogen is low in most natural forest ecosystems, most trees grow reasonably well and are acceptably green. By slowing their growth rate, trees can maintain healthy looking foliage. Furthermore, trees grow in response to their environment. They adjust their root:shoot ratios to provide adequate nutrients. For instance, in a fertile soil, tree roots occupy a smaller volume of soil but are more greatly branched. By comparison, their canopies are larger than their root systems. On the other hand, roots on trees in less fertile soils occupy a greater soil volume; they are longer and less branched. The root systems of such trees are comparatively larger than their canopies, which helps compensate for reduced mineral availability.

Slow to moderate growth is normal and desirable for most trees. In fact, studies have shown that resistance to certain insects and diseases decreases in rapidly growing trees

and that such trees are more nutritionally suitable to some pests. When growing conditions are not restrictive, much of the available energy is shifted to growth. On the other hand, when conditions restrict growth, more energy is diverted for defense. Trees under low to moderate stress produce higher levels of defensive (pest-inhibiting) chemicals.

Undiagnosed nutrient imbalance problem.

Symptoms of nitrogen deficiency are relatively rare in urban and rural trees. Perceptible nitrogen deficiencies are most prevalent in sandy or silty soils low in organic matter and in poorly drained soils. Deficiencies also may develop on sites where the soil organic matter is gradually depleted by regular removal of leaf litter or by competing vegetation and crops (fruit and nuts).

Soil nitrogen is contained primarily in organic matter. Soil organisms gradually decompose this material, releasing small amounts of water-soluble nitrate ions (NO_3^-) and ammonium ions (NH_4^+). Most of the ammonium ions are adsorbed (weakly held) on soil colloids or fixed (strongly held) within clay particles. By comparison, most of the nitrate ions are free in the soil water, where they are readily available for plant uptake but subject to leaching by heavy irrigation or rain.

There is a small input of nitrogen from the atmosphere, and certain soil microorganisms can fix (convert) elemental nitrogen from the air to forms that can be absorbed by plants. Some nitrogen-fixing organisms are free-living in the soil while others occur in specialized root nodules of various plants.

Appreciable amounts of nitrates (from acid-forming, nitrogen-based air pollutants) are deposited on the soil by rain and snow. Lightning also fixes smaller quantities of nitrates, which are carried by the rain to the soil.

The new leaves of trees with severe nitrogen deficiency are typically smaller than normal but appear relatively green. The older leaves, however, are yellow. The mobility of nitrogen in the plant allows it to move from the older to the new, developing foliage. Nitrogen deficiency can be corrected by adding nitrogen-based fertilizer.

Phosphorus and Potassium

Levels of phosphorus (P) and potassium (K) usually are sufficient in most soils for normal tree growth. Potassium, however, may be deficient in subsoils, especially those low in organic matter. Even though the level of phosphorus may be low in some soils, mychorrhizal fungi aid in its absorption. Phosphorus does not move readily in the soil and tends to be found close to the surface in organic matter. It also forms insoluble salts in strongly acid or alkaline soils and thus is largely unavailable.

Adding a 2- to 3-inch layer of organic material (mulch) over the root zone can help gradually eliminate deficiencies in nitrogen, phosphorus, and potassium. Besides providing essential elements upon breakdown, organic material can lower soil pH, improving the availability of certain nutrients. Mulching also encourages soil microbial activity (mycorrhizae and nitrogen-fixing bacteria), which increases the availability of nutrients. It also improves soil structure, moderates soil temperature extremes, reduces erosion, and conserves soil moisture.

Iron

Iron often is unavailable in alkaline and or poorly drained soils. The symptoms of iron deficiency are just the opposite of those of nitrogen deficiency. Young leaves are yellow (with green veins), while older leaves remain darker green. Leaf size is also reduced. Iron deficiency can sometimes be corrected by lowering soil pH with sulfur, or more gradually by mulching the soil surface with leaf litter and wood chips or green waste.

Determining Whether to Fertilize

Young trees need increasing supplies of minerals to grow well. Nutrient demand is usually met when root growth and soil volume are unrestricted and the soil is relatively fertile or if fertilizer is applied. Young trees growing in relatively fertile soil seldom need to be fertilized and often don't respond to moderate fertilization. However, those growing in infertile soils usually will grow more quickly with the addition of fertilizer.

Mature trees, on the other hand, can adapt to reduced soil fertility by slowing growth. However, moderate to severe nutrient deficiency can cause abnormalities and poor growth. Moderately slow growth in mature trees generally is normal and desirable. As trees grow larger, demand for minerals, particularly nitrogen, to maintain growth and life functions increases, while availability decreases as minerals are increasingly bound in living and dead tissue. Thus, nutrient availability may not be able to satisfy the demand of large, old trees. Such trees may benefit from moderate fertilization, but the overstimulation of mature trees with fertilizer can result in excessive growth, reduced drought resistance, susceptibility to certain pests and diseases (such as aphids, mites, psyllids, and fireblight), and additional maintenance costs. Trees stressed by such problems as drought, poor soil aeration, inadequate light, or root disease usually do not respond to fertilization unless these factors are mitigated.

To summarize, fertilization is appropriate for reasons such as these:
- to promote growth in young, established trees when needed (newly planted trees may not respond to fertilization for several years)
- to compensate for restricted nutrient cycling caused by pavement, tree litter removal, turf, competitive ground covers, and other events
- to correct mineral deficiencies
- to promote and maintain moderate growth in trees growing in nutrient-poor soils

- to maintain health and appearance of mature trees (but remember that rapid growth may be undesirable)
- to encourage root development in transplanted or root-injured trees.

Using Fertilizer

Analysis and Testing

Soil analysis is not always a reliable means to determine nutrient imbalances in trees because critical values have not been determined for many species of trees. Soil chemistry varies with location, depth, time of year, moisture content, and other factors. Chemical analysis, if requested, can determine toxic levels of boron, chloride, sodium, and total salinity, as well as pH. Any soil test is only as good as the sample, though, so samples should be taken from at least four quadrants in the outer one-third of the tree's drip zone.

Leaf analysis can be used to determine mineral level; however, as with soil analysis, critical levels have not been established for many tree species. Interpretation of results is difficult at best, but leaf analysis can be useful if both healthy and symptomatic trees are sampled for comparison.

Water can contribute toxic levels of mineral elements, so it is recommended that water be tested as well.

Forms of Nitrogen

Tree roots can absorb nitrogen as nitrate (NO_3^-) and ammonium (NH_4^+) ions, and directly as urea $(NH_2)_2CO$. Nitrate nitrogen, when added in a water-soluble form, is subject to leaching because there are relatively

Stunted growth on *Liquidambar* from iron chlorosis.

few anion exchange sites on the colloidal particles of most soils. Thus, nitrate ions move readily in the soil water. Loss is greatest when plants are heavily irrigated.

Ammonium ions and urea are soluble but are retained primarily in the soil. Both tend to acidify the soil. Ammonium ions are converted by soil organisms to nitrate ions within several weeks. This reaction is dependent on soil temperature, soil aeration, pH, and the activity of soil organisms.

Urea is converted to ammonium ions and then to nitrate ions. Some ions may be lost to volatilization in alkaline or sandy soil. Ammonium-based fertilizers and urea should be watered in to reduce volatilization. Ammonium ions are more available in cold soil, while nitrate ions are more available in warm soil.

Application Rates

One to six pounds of actual nitrogen per 1,000 square feet of drip line is routinely recommended for shade and ornamental trees. The lower rate is ideal for slower-growing

Iron chlorosis of *Liquidambar* in alkaline soil.

and mature trees. A moderate rate (2 to 3 pounds) appears best for young, established, and fast-growing trees. Fertilization with more than 4 pounds of nitrogen is rarely warranted, and lower rates are more commonly recommended. Overfertilization can injure plants, increase pest problems, reduce drought tolerance, increase maintenance costs, and contaminate the groundwater.

The selected materials should be applied to the root zone. Because much of the tree's root system is concentrated within an area 1.5 times the size of the drip line (edge of leafy canopy), fertilizing that area is usually adequate. The numbers printed on a bag of fertilizer (for example, 30-10-7) indicate the relative percentage by weight of nitrogen, phosphorus, and potassium (in that order) contained in the bag. A 60-pound bag of ammonium sulfate contains 21 percent nitrogen as stated on the label. Therefore, 1 pound of the material contains 0.21 pounds of nitrogen. To apply 2 pounds of nitrogen per 1,000 square feet of root zone, 9.5 pounds of fertilizer should be used:

$$2 \text{ lb per } 1,000 \text{ ft}^2 \div 21/100 =$$
$$2 \div 0.21 =$$
$$9.5 \text{ lb per } 1,000 \text{ ft}^2$$

If the tree has a 60-foot spread and fertilizer is to be applied to an area with a radius of 1.5 times the drip line, how much fertilizer is needed?

Area of a circle = πr^2 ($\pi = 3.14$)
Radius of root zone to be fertilized = 60/2
  = 30 ft $\times$ 1.5 = 45 ft
Area of root zone = 3.14 (45 ft^2) = 6,359 ft^2
Amount to add = 9.5 lb of product per
  1,000 ft^2 $\times$ 6,358 ft^2 = 60.4 lb

Application Timing

Most spring growth (leaf flush, flowers, fruit set, and shoot elongation) is accomplished with energy and nutrients stored the previous season. Fertilizer applied just before or at the onset of growth is incorporated in new tissue to only a limited extent. Most of the added nutrients will be used for next season's growth.

Although fertilizer may be applied at any time, it may not be readily absorbed or assimilated, and it may not stimulate growth until the following season. In most deciduous trees, shoot initials are formed in

---

SOURCES OF NITROGEN AND OTHER MATERIALS

Inorganic, *water soluble* for quick release

calcium nitrate	ammonium sulfate
ammonium nitrate	monoammonium phosphate
potassium nitrate	diammonium phosphate
potassium chloride	potassium sulfate
potassium nitrate	superphosphate (single/triple)

Organic, *water insoluble*, converted by soil organisms (slow release)

manures	sludge
grape pomace	seaweed
bone meal	dried blood
cover crops	cottonseed meal
tankage	fish meal, emulsion
compost	

Synthetic organic, *water soluble* or converted by soil organisms or by hydrolysis

urea (rapidly soluble in water)
sulfur coated urea* (slowly soluble)
urea formaldehyde* (slowly soluble)
isobutyl diurea* (slowly soluble)
*These slow-release fertilizers are ideal for sandy soils, which drain quickly and have a low cation exchange capacity.

FORMULATIONS

Encapsulated: sulfur- or resin-coated urea; can be broadcast or incorporated.
Granular: dry, pulverized; ideal for broadcasting or incorporating.
Preformed: spikes, tabs, pellets, briquettes; premeasured, convenient, more expensive, poor distribution.
Complete: contains nitrogen (N), phosphate (P_2O_5), and potash (K_2O).
Complete + minors: contains N, P, K + micronutrients (for example, Fe, Zn).

APPLICATION METHODS

Broadcast: fertilizer is surface applied in dry or liquid form.
Liquid soil injection: often used to fertilize trees in lawns; solution is applied 4 to 12 inches deep.
Fertigation: fertilizer is metered in irrigation water.
Foliar: applied to foliage; best for micronutrients; is temporary and does not solve underlying problems.
Incorporation: fertilizer is added to backfill, cultivated in, or placed in augered holes in soil.
Trunk injection: fertilizer solution is injected into holes made in the trunk; injurious and temporary; does not solve the underlying problem; is effective only for micronutrients. It is impractical to inject a sufficient amount of N, P, or K in this manner.
Implants: dry plugs are inserted into holes in the tree; injurious and temporary.

---

the terminal and lateral bud before dormancy. Shoot growth ends the following season once the initials fully expand. Many trees will continue shoot elongation as long as soil and environmental conditions are favorable. Although improved growing conditions brought about by fertilization may result in longer shoots and larger, greener leaves, no new buds will form until the following season.

Traditional wisdom recommends applying fertilizer in the late fall because roots

Open Discussion on Fertilizer at the Fertilization Symposium

By Alan Siewert

Following the presentations at the tree and shrub fertilizer conference in Akron, Ohio, held in May 2000, the participants and presenters were asked to consider the following two questions: Is there a statement about fertilizer you are confident in making? and Which questions do you have about fertilizer?

The purpose of these questions was to stimulate and direct discussion on the subject. The closest the group came to consensus was that fertilizer is only one tool and should be used on a case-by-case basis in connection with other health care treatments.

Discussion on a second point, "Fertilizer is more effective in nutrient-deficient soil than in nutrient-sufficient soils," ran into a snag when the question "What is good soil?" was brought up. Three presenters had evidence to suggest that fertilizer results were more apparent on poor sites than on good sites; however, the lack of information about soil characteristics prior to the studies made comparisons difficult and prevented consensus on this point.

Further discussion centered on movement of nitrogen in the soil, leaching of minerals into groundwater, and effects of fertilization on the susceptibility of plants to pest problems. Examples of research results were debated, and there was agreement about the need for more research in these areas.

RECOMMENDATION FOR FUTURE RESEARCH

The final exercise of the program was to brainstorm ideas for future research.

The assembled group believed that the following basic protocols for future research will benefit the industry and improve the information produced by the research:

1. Soil characteristics should be ascertained to establish a baseline for the test. The soil's chemical, physical, and biological properties should be tested using standardized methods and reported in the final publication of the experiment.
2. Research should be done on sites more characteristic of what the arborist deals with in the real world. The group felt that much of the data presented were from environments different from what they work in. There was concern that the use of information from nursery sites or old farm fields may not be applicable to urban or suburban planting sites.

Participants believe that the following areas of research are needed (ranked in order of most important to least important):

1. soil physical and biological properties and how they relate to nutrient availability and tree health
2. leaching and nitrogen behavior in the soil
3. measuring success of a treatment
4. indicators of a healthy tree
5. long-term site and soil studies
6. optimal timing for fertilizer applications to benefit the tree
7. determining how much fertilizer to use, which kind to apply, and in which situations
8. correlating soil fertility to soil tests and the response of the tree
9. how to manage, fertilize, and measure the success of the treatments on a mature tree
10. compiling a comprehensive list of trees and their specific needs for and reactions to fertilizer

Fertilization as a practice has a tremendous amount of variability. Material formulation; application methods and timing; species response; existing soil chemical, physical, and biological characteristics; pest reaction; and other factors influence the success or failure of a fertilizer treatment. These factors create a matrix of variables that we have only begun to examine with scientific research.

The fertilizer symposium provided results on specific variables in this matrix, but much of the arborist's fieldwork remains unstudied. Arborists must rely on their skills and experience to extrapolate from the existing research to arrive at field recommendations for each situation.

The results and recommendations of this group should help direct research to continue to fill in the gaps of information.

are still growing and winter rain will carry the nutrients to the roots where they will be absorbed and made available for growth the following spring. Metabolic demand and nitrogen uptake, however, are low during the dormant season. Consequently, readily soluble forms of nitrogen applied in the winter are subject to leaching and degradation. Studies indicate that nitrogen uptake peaks during the spring and summer, coinciding with the period of greatest nitrogen demand.

Late summer and early fall appear to be effective application times to make nitrogen available for growth in the spring. Conditions are favorable for nutrient uptake and storage: Shoot growth has stopped, root growth is increasing, energy stores are high, the weather is cooling, and moisture is more available. Early spring applications may be effective also because of increased root development and favorable moisture conditions, and because there is enough time for nutrient storage.

Caution: Mineral Salts

The movement of water into and out of root cells is largely dependent on the concentration of solutes (ions) in the surrounding soil. Excess salts from overfertilization or saline water can cause water stress, induced by the osmotic properties of salts. Normally, the mineral content within root cells is greater than that of the surrounding soil water. When the concentration of minerals is greater on one side of a semipermeable membrane (cell wall), water moves across

Marginal leaf burn caused by overfertilization.

the membrane until equilibrium has been reached. This process is called *osmosis*. When the concentration of salts in the surrounding soil water is greater than that within tree roots, water flow will reverse direction and flow out of the root cells (*reverse osmosis*). This process results in loss of internal cellular pressure (*plasmolysis*), cellular damage, foliar wilt, and marginal leaf burn. The absorption of excess salts also can have a toxic effect. Unless soil conditions are corrected, affected trees may grow poorly or die. Where water quality and quantity are not limiting, salts can be leached from the soil by irrigation.

Salt index is a measure of the potential for a fertilizer to cause burn (raise the osmotic pressure of the soil solution, drawing water out of root cells and the plant). It is also a measure of the rate of dissociation of the fertilizer into its ions. Fertilizers with low salt indexes are less likely to leach, burn, or cause salt buildup. The total salt effect of a fertilizer depends on the rate applied and the nature of the fertilizer. Slow-release fertilizers have a lower salt index because they release ions slowly.

Conclusion

Few trees are well adapted to soils commonly found in urban areas. As a result, many trees grow poorly, suffer pest problems, decline progressively, and die prematurely. Major problems include compacted soil (poor aeration, water penetration), limited soil volume, poor drainage (poor aeration), drought, high pH, exposed soil, lack of mulching, low soil organic matter content, competition with other vegetation, and

impervious pavement. Rather than diagnose the cause of poor tree growth, arborists and landscape specialists often resort to fertilizers to solve problems. Soil nutrition often isn't the chief concern. Greater attention must be placed on the diagnosis and mitigation of factors contributing to stress. Many tree problems could be avoided by improved tree selection, appropriate site selection and preparation, proper planting techniques, and good maintenance.

Fertilization, obviously, is an important tool in urban tree care. It can be used to promote growth in young trees and normal growth in mature trees where soil nutrition is limiting. Unless a mineral deficiency exists, fertilization is largely unwarranted. The routine use of fertilizer as cheap insurance, without proper diagnosis, could injure plants and contaminate ground- and surface water; it is also expensive.

Bruce Hagen is an urban forester with the California Department of Forestry in Santa Rosa, California.

TEST QUESTIONS

To receive continuing education unit (CEU) credit (1.5 CEU) for home study of this article, after you have read it, darken the appropriate circles on the answer form in the back of this book. **Be sure to use the answer form that corresponds to this article.** Each question has only one correct answer. A passing score for this test is 80 percent. Photocopies of the answer form are **not** acceptable.

After you have answered the questions on the answer form, complete the registration information on the form and send it to ISA, P.O. Box 3129, Champaign, IL 61826-3129.

You will be notified only if you do not pass. CEU codes for the exams you have passed will appear on your CEU updates. If you do not pass, you have the option of taking the test as often as necessary.

1. Excess fertilization can cause the following harmful effects **except**
   a. reduced water-holding capacity of soil
   b. groundwater contamination
   c. restricted root development
   d. foliage burn

2. Trees obtain energy by
   a. trapping mineral nutrients
   b. developing root hairs
   c. converting nitrogen
   d. converting light energy

3. Nearly all elements are absorbed from the soil water as
   a. organic matter
   b. fertilizers
   c. charged particles
   d. glucose

4. Cations adsorbed to soil particles resist
   a. anions
   b. bonding to soil colloids
   c. leaching
   d. decomposition

5. Microbial activity releases bound mineral ions during which process?
   a. cation exchange
   b. organic matter decomposition
   c. hydrolysis
   d. photosynthesis

6. In strongly alkaline soils
   a. some minerals are unavailable
   b. soil particles may be poorly aggregated
   c. excess salts may also be a problem
   d. all of the above

7. Strongly acid soils have
   a. decreased solubility of manganese
   b. increased soil bacterial activity
   c. low microbial activity
   d. all of the above

8. The cation exchange capacity (CEC) indicates a soil's ability to
   a. hold minerals
   b. leach cations
   c. absorb anions
   d. volatilize nutrients

9. The CEC of a soil depends largely on the content of
   a. positively charged particles
   b. anions in the soil
   c. clay and organic matter
   d. alkaline minerals

10. Anions, which carry a negative charge, are less likely to be adsorbed by colloidal particles, and are more subject to leaching.
    a. true
    b. false

11. When gypsum is added to sodic soils, Na^{++} is replaced with Ca^{++}, thereby
    a. increasing alkalinity
    b. increasing sodium
    c. reducing acidity
    d. reducing alkalinity

12. Nitrogen provides the most universal response in plant growth because it is the most
    a. bound mineral nutrient
    b. organic mineral nutrient
    c. abundant mineral nutrient in soil
    d. limiting mineral nutrient in the soil

13. To compensate for reduced mineral availability in soils with low fertility, roots will
    a. be shorter and highly branched
    b. have a low dry-weight mass
    c. occupy a large soil volume
    d. occupy a smaller soil volume

14. Perceptible nitrogen deficiencies might occur in
    a. poorly drained soil
    b. soil low in organic matter
    c. soil from which leaf litter is removed regularly
    d. all of the above

15. Severe nitrogen deficiency is typified by
    a. normal new leaves; smaller older leaves
    b. smaller new leaves; yellow older leaves
    c. yellow new leaves; normal older leaves
    d. yellow new leaves; yellow older leaves

16. Iron deficiency symptoms are typified by
    a. reduced leaf size
    b. older leaves remaining dark
    c. yellow young leaves
    d. all of the above

17. To reduce volatilization of ammonium-based fertilizer,
    a. always apply it to the soil surface
    b. keep the fertilized area dry
    c. avoid its use on alkaline soil
    d. water it in

18. Overstimulating mature trees with a high-nitrogen fertilizer could result in which of the following?
    a. additional maintenance costs
    b. increased pest problems
    c. reduced drought resistance
    d. all of the above

19. According to this article, which is the recommended rate of actual nitrogen per 1,000 square feet of drip zone for young established and fast-growing trees?
    a. 0 to 2 pounds
    b. 2 to 3 pounds
    c. 4 to 6 pounds
    d. 6 to 8 pounds

20. Which term is applied to the process that causes wilt when water flows out of root cells and into the surrounding soils?
    a. reverse osmosis or plasmolysis
    b. osmosis or plasmolysis
    c. leaching
    d. cation exchange

21. Fertilizer with a low salt index is less likely to
    a. burn
    b. cause salt buildup
    c. leach
    d. all of the above

22. Fertilizer applied during the current growth season may be most visible in
    a. dormancy
    b. the following year
    c. new bud development
    d. all of the above

23. If you had a 40-pound bag of 10-10-10 fertilizer and you wanted to apply 2 pounds of nitrogen per 1,000 square feet, you would need to use
    a. 0.5 bags per 1,000 square feet
    b. 2 bags per 1,000 square feet
    c. 4 bags per 1,000 square feet
    d. 6 bags per 1,000 square feet

24. Soil analysis is a good method to determine
    a. presence of mychorrhizal fungi
    b. levels of certain mineral elements
    c. when to fertilize
    d. all of the above

25. Urea is an example of which source of nitrogen fertilizer?
    a. water insoluble, inorganic
    b. water insoluble, organic
    c. water soluble, inorganic
    d. water soluble, synthetic organic

26. Soil pH affects the solubility of minerals and thus their availability to plants.
    a. true
    b. false

27. Mature trees can adapt to reduced soil fertility by slowing growth.
    a. true
    b. false

28. The process in which nitrogen is converted into its gaseous form and lost into the atmosphere is
    a. fixation
    b. mineralization
    c. denitrification
    d. volatilization

29. Most nitrogen is taken up by plants in the form of
    a. fixed elemental nitrogen
    b. ammonium ions
    c. nitrogen gas
    d. nitrate ions

30. The level of phosphorus and potassium is sufficient in most soils for normal tree growth.
    a. true
    b. false

SLOW- OR CONTROLLED-RELEASE FERTILIZERS

By Roger C. Funk

A slow- or controlled-release fertilizer contains essential elements in a form that delays initial availability or that extends availability over time. Most slow-release fertilizers contain only nitrogen in this form because it is actively leached as nitrate (NO_3) from mineral soils and also can be lost through volatilization when surface-applied. Additional elements may be included in slow-release form, primarily for use in containers with soilless media or other situations in which leaching may be a problem. Typically, a controlled-release fertilizer is delivered either through modification of the fertilizer product, such as coating or encapsulation, or through the inherent water insolubility of synthetic or natural organic polymers. Recently, short-chain soluble organic polymers have become available that also are considered a controlled-release source of nitrogen. In addition, inhibitors are available that do not slow the availability of nitrogen but rather slow transformation to forms that are lost through leaching or volatilization. Controlled-release fertilizers generally cost more than quick-release sources, such as urea, but they offer several advantages that contribute to their increasing popularity. These advantages include

- reduced labor costs associated with fertilization because the number of applications is generally reduced
- reduced risk of root cell plasmolysis (fertilizer burn)
- a more uniform supply of nitrogen provided to the plant
- less potential for leaching, volatilization, and denitrification of nitrogen
- more efficient utilization of nitrogen by plants

Private and university testing often provide a mechanism of choosing products to

Learning objectives—
The arborist will be able to

- explain the advantages of slow- or controlled-release fertilizers.
- describe various types of slow release fertilizers and how they work.

meet nitrogen-release criteria; however, there is no method to compare the cost per unit of nutrient per unit of time among the various controlled-release fertilizers. Until a simplified method is developed to compare costs among these materials, selection will continue to be based on subjective initial screening to meet application criteria, followed by comparison of cost on a unit–nutrient basis, on a unit–volume basis, or both.

Table 1 compares the approximate availability period for nitrogen fertilizers.

COATED FERTILIZERS

There are generally three types of coatings that contain soluble fertilizer, which is released when the coating is broken down:

- Semipermeable membranes allow water to diffuse into the granule and

increase internal osmotic pressure which breaks the membrane.
- Impermeable membranes with small pores swell as water diffuses into the granule, allowing the dissolved salts through the enlarged pores.
- Impermeable membranes are degraded by chemical, physical, and/or microbial action.

Sulfur-Coated Urea (SCU)

Sulfur-coated urea consists of a urea particle coated with a sulfur layer that has imperfections ranging in size from pin holes to cracks. As water enters through the imperfections, urea dissolves and diffuses into the soil solution. Ideally, nitrogen is released slowly, depending upon the size and number of imperfections. Nitrogen can be released all at once, however, when the sulfur shell cracks at its weakest point. Some SCU products have a wax layer on the outside to seal the imperfections and keep the particles from breaking down prematurely. With those products, the wax first must be broken down by soil microbes before water enters through the imperfections in the sulfur. The rate of nitrogen release is expressed as a seven-day dissolution rate, which is the percentage of urea that dissolves at 100°F. The more rapid the dissolution rate, the more water-soluble nitrogen available.

Table 1. Nitrogen fertilizers and their corresponding availability period.

Type of nitrogen fertilizer	Availability period
soluble, quick-release	6 to 8 weeks
soluble, slowly available	8 to 16 weeks
insoluble, slowly available	1 to 3 years
coated or encapsulated	2 to 12 months

Polymer-Coated Materials

Until recently, the extra-thick coating needed to ensure consistent, long-term, controlled release was costly to produce. New technology, however, allows sustained release with an ultrathin polymer layer.

Two general types of poly-coated nitrogen fertilizers are available: polymer-coated urea (sometimes called reactive layer coated urea) and polymer-coated, sulfur-coated urea. With both types, nitrogen availability continues over a 2 to 12 month period, compared to 6 to 8 weeks for urea.

Nitrogen becomes available from polymer-coated urea as water diffuses through the coating and dissolves the urea particles. Temperature and coating thickness affect how quickly elements diffuse through the coating. Low temperatures and a thick coating slow diffusion.

For poly-coated SCU, water passes first through the polymer coating, then through the sulfur coating.

Slowly Available, Insoluble Fertilizers

These fertilizers are natural and synthetic organics that contain both soluble and insoluble fractions. The bulk of the synthetic organics are nitrogen fertilizers produced with several of the aldehydes. Natural organics are byproducts from processing animal or vegetable matter, and they contain essential elements of value as fertilizers.

Isobutylidene Diurea (IBDU)

IBDU is a synthetic organic fertilizer that releases nitrogen through the hydrolytic action of water. Large granules have less surface area per volume than do small granules; they release nitrogen more slowly because IBDU must contact water for nitrogen release to occur.

Unlike with other organic fertilizers, nitrogen release continues during cold weather. In addition to particle size, lower soil pH and high soil moisture increase nitrogen release.

Urea Formaldehyde (UF)

UF was the first synthetic organic fertilizer, and it remains the most common. Reacting urea with formaldehyde yields some unreacted urea with various urea–polymer chains

of varying lengths, depending on the reaction conditions. All longer-chained methylene ureas are water insoluble and depend on microbial decomposition for release of nitrogen. Factors such as soil temperatures, moisture, pH, and aeration influence the breakdown of UF through their influence on microbial activity. With UF (and in contrast to IBDU), cold weather slows down nitrogen release, and particle size is not a significant factor. The nitrogen in UF is classified into water-soluble and water-insoluble fractions.

- **Water-soluble nitrogen** dissolves in cold water at 68°F to 77°F. This fraction is usually about 30 percent of a typical UF product and contains unreacted urea and short-chain polymers.
- **Water-insoluble nitrogen (WIN)** comprises cold-water-insoluble (CWIN) and hot-water-insoluble (HWIN) nitrogen. CWIN is insoluble in cold water but soluble in hot (212°F) water. These medium-length chains represent about 40 percent of the nitrogen in UF.

Hot-water-insoluble nitrogen has the longest chains and provides the longest residual activity.

Natural Organics

Natural organic fertilizers were once the only available fertilizer. When synthetic processes were developed, these new fertilizers became popular because they were less expensive per nutrient-unit with lower application rates.

An increase in environmental awareness and concern for "chemicals" has renewed interest in natural organics. As with synthetic organics, nitrogen release relies on microbial decomposition.

Slowly Available, Soluble Fertilizers

Certain soluble compounds such as short-chain UF reaction products and triazone release nitrogen at significantly slower rates than urea and are considered slowly available sources of nitrogen by the Association of American Plant Food Control Officials (AAPFCO). Both materials also contain unreacted urea, which provides quick-release nitrogen.

Inhibitors

Inhibitors do not slow the solubility of nitrogen compounds. Instead, they slow the transformation to forms that are lost through leaching or volatilization.

Nitrification inhibitors reduce the bacteria responsible for the conversion process by which ammonium is converted to nitrate in the soil. Inhibition keeps nitrogen in the ammonium form, which is less subject to losses by leaching than nitrate.

Urease inhibitors inactivate the soil enzyme urease, which promotes rapid hydrolysis of urea to ammonia. Rapid hydrolysis is particularly important when applying urea to the soil surface, where normal losses through volatilization average about 15 to 20 percent.

Roger Funk is vice president and general manager of the Davey Institute, the research and development division of The Davey Tree Expert Company, in Kent, Ohio.

TEST QUESTIONS

To receive continuing education unit (CEU) credit (.5 CEU) for home study of this article, after you have read it, darken the appropriate circles on the answer form in the back of this book. **Be sure to use the answer form that corresponds to this article.** Each question has only one correct answer. A passing score for this test is 80 percent. Photocopies of the answer form are **not** acceptable.

After you have answered the questions on the answer form, complete the registration information on the form and send it to ISA, P.O. Box 3129, Champaign, IL 61826-3129.

You will be notified only if you do not pass. CEU codes for the exams you have passed will appear on your CEU updates. If you do not pass, you have the option of taking the test as often as necessary.

1. Slow- or controlled-release fertilizer reduces the potential for nitrogen loss through leaching or volatilization.
   a. true
   b. false

2. A controlled-release fertilizer usually contains which primary nutrient?
   a. potassium
   b. phosphorus
   c. nitrogen
   d. magnesium

3. Which of the following nitrogen fertilizers could have the granule broken into smaller pieces without significantly affecting the period of availability in the soil?
   a. urea formaldehyde
   b. polymer-coated urea
   c. isobutylidene diurea
   d. sulfur-coated urea

4. Which of the following fertilizers is considered a quick-release source of nitrogen?
   a. urea
   b. urea formaldehyde
   c. triazone
   d. isobutylidene diurea

5. Nitrification inhibitors
   a. slow the transformation of nitrogen to forms that are leached or volatilized
   b. slow the solubility of nitrogen compounds
   c. form an impermeable coating around fertilizer particles
   d. inhibit the absorption of nitrogen by plants

6. Only fertilizers insoluble in water are considered slowly available sources of nitrogen by the American Association of Plant Food Control Officials (AAPFCO).
   a. true
   b. false

7. Compared to quick-release fertilizers, controlled-release fertilizers offer which of the following advantages?
   a. reduced risk of cell plasmolysis (fertilizer burn)
   b. less expensive
   c. less potential for leaching, volatilization, and denitrification of nitrogen
   d. both a and c

8. Natural organic fertilizers generally cost more (per nutrient-unit) and require higher application rates than either synthetic organic or inorganic fertilizers.
   a. true
   b. false

9. The fraction of urea formaldehyde that provides the longest residual is
   a. cold-water soluble
   b. cold-water insoluble
   c. hot-water insoluble
   d. unreacted urea

10. Nitrogen release from coated urea fertilizer is expressed by the
    a. water-insoluble nitrogen (WIN)
    b. dissolution rate
    c. percentage of nitrogen
    d. membrane permeability

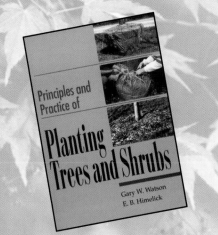

FLOOD-DAMAGED TREES

By Kim D. Coder

Courtesy of IL Dept. of Natural Resources

Floods destroy trees, disrupt essential resource availability, and change the surrounding environment. Once floods are past, recovery can be a slow process. Flooding forces a host of external and internal changes onto trees. A clearer understanding of how trees react to, and how their essential resources are changed by, flooding can help us better care for trees.

What Are Floods?

A flood is the saturation and inundation of soil with water. The water can be stagnant and standing or rapidly flowing. Floods can occur in the cold, dormant winter period or at the height of hot summer weather. Floods can be quick, passing in days, or may be part of a long-term change in the environment, lasting for several years. Floods can be from freshwater flows above and below ground or from saltwater tides and storm surges.

Tree survival of floods depends on many attributes of the tree, site, and flood. The extent and destructiveness of flooding on tree growth depends on flood duration; the time of year flooding occurred; water quality and water oxygen content; water depth; air and water temperature; and tree stage of

Learning objectives— The arborist will be able to

- describe the internal and external effects on trees under flooded conditions.
- be familiar with the importance of oxygen to a tree root system and surrounding soil.
- be familiar with the chemical changes that affect trees and soil during floods.
- describe the actions necessary to minimize tree and site damage after a flood.

life, structure, and health. There is no single kind of flood or flood damage. In this article, only temporary, freshwater inundation and associated tree damage are reviewed.

Drowning Trees

Flood damage to trees develops in four primary ways:

1. acute soil and tree changes because of saturated or inundated soil conditions
2. floodwater delivery and deposition of organics, sediments, chemicals, and other materials to the tree area
3. floodwater flow physically knocking over and mechanically damaging trees or scouring soil away from the rooting area
4. chronic problems associated with a changing environment and modified tree reactivity

Probably the most limiting, and most immediate, aspect of flooding on trees and their essential resources is the lack of oxygen to roots and soil. Poor aeration of the root zone and the suffocation of living tissues generate many direct and indirect problems. Understanding how oxygen is used by the tree and in the soil can help direct preservation and maintenance activities.

"Breathing Oxygen"

Oxygen is critical to aerobic life forms. Why do trees (and humans) need oxygen? Oxygen acts as an electron acceptor. The tree "hands off" electrons to oxygen. The flow of electrons from high concentrations inside the tree to low concentrations in the atmosphere allows aerobic life to survive. This biological process is called respiration. For every 18°F increase in temperature above 40°F, respiration doubles (Table 1.)

Trees need oxygen to live. This need can be a problem for trees because they have

Table 1. Relative temperature effects on oxygen saturation in floodwater, carbohydrate use in the tree under ideal conditions, and carbohydrate use in the tree under oxygen-poor conditions. (2X means two times the respiration rate at 40°F under aerated conditions. *signifies production of materials such as ethanol that could build up to toxic levels.)

Temperature	Relative Maximum Oxygen Concentration in Flood Water	Relative Amount of Carbohydrate Used in Respiration (+O_2)	Relative Amount of Carbohydrate Used in Respiration (–O_2)
32°F	1.14	—	—
40°F	1.00	X	20X*
58°F	0.79	2X	40X*
76°F	0.66	4X	80X*
94°F	0.57	8X	160X*

no circulatory system to carry oxygen to every cell. Every tree cell must be able to capture oxygen on its own. From the highest shoot tip to the farthest reach of the root tips, every part of the tree must have oxygen.

Using oxygen from the atmosphere can be difficult for stems, leaves, and roots. Most woody parts of a tree have waterproof bark. Bark has gas-exchange openings called lenticels. Tree leaves are thin but are covered with a protective wax coating. The leaf has valves (stomates) that open to allow gas exchange. Tree roots are in a terrible spot for capturing oxygen.

Root Plight
Roots are in a moist, dark soil environment that has many sizes of pores. Small-sized pores between the solid minerals are filled with water. Large-sized soil pores are filled with air. These large, interconnected, air-filled pores allow oxygen to move into the soil and to the roots. Oxygen can then be used for root respiration. As soils become compacted or wet, more pores hold water and fewer contain air.

The soil is filled with tree roots plus the roots of other plants in the area. In addition, roots are surrounded with millions of soil-living organisms, most of which need oxygen to live. A healthy, moist soil with all of these living organisms consumes much oxygen. A flood at growing-season temperatures can cause all available oxygen to be used up within a few hours. Then the only area where oxygen is available is in the top 1/10 inch of soil that is in contact with oxygenated water.

Microbes act as oxygen sponges, using any available oxygen quickly. Because the microbes are throughout the soil, especially surrounding tree roots, they grab oxygen before tree roots can do so. As oxygen is consumed, respiration using other materials such as nitrogen, manganese, iron, sulfur, and carbon begins.

Dealing with Electrons
The normal atmosphere surrounding the top of a tree is filled with about 21 percent oxygen. Healthy soil atmospheres are highly variable, but many contain 8 to 15 percent oxygen. A tree needs to lose electrons easily to the environment to survive. Oxygen is an element that behaves as if it has a low number of electrons. To make energy to live, a tree offers electrons to oxygen. The electron-hungry oxygen quickly takes electrons away.

As long as there is plenty of oxygen, the food produced by photosynthesis can be quickly and efficiently converted into work-producing energy. If oxygen becomes limited under flooded soil conditions, respiration becomes more difficult. As soil pores fill with water, oxygen movement is greatly reduced. Once air pore space drops below about 10 percent of all pores in a soil, oxygen movement slows rapidly. When all pores are water filled, oxygen movement is slowed to the roots by more than 7,000 times normal rates.

The effect of flooded soils is to suffocate tree roots. Water in the soil limits the movement of oxygen to the roots. The soil organisms and roots quickly use up all available oxygen, causing anaerobic ("no oxygen") conditions. Lack of oxygen means tree root problems.

Alternative Lifestyles
When oxygen is missing in flooded soils, other elements or materials are used by soil organisms as electron acceptors. Nitrogen is the first major element used for respiration by soil microbes when oxygen is depleted. Nitrogen respiration in warm, saturated soils can cause available nitrogen from fertilizers to be turned into inert gas within a few days.

With no oxygen, and nitrogen respiration getting started in the soil, the next element to be used for respiration by microbes is manganese. Manganese is normally insoluble in a soil. When manganese is used for respiration, it becomes very soluble and mobile. This change in manganese can be toxic to roots. Newly mobile manganese may be taken up into the tree, poisoning the shoot.

As saturated soil conditions continue with no oxygen present, and nitrogen and manganese are used up as electron acceptors, iron becomes a respiration element. Iron respiration allows insoluble forms of iron to be changed into soluble forms. Like manganese, soluble iron can produce many toxicity problems.

Hitting Electron Equilibrium
After a time, cells have trouble transferring electrons to the environment because the concentration of electrons both inside and outside the tree is about the same. Sulfur becomes the next element used by soil organisms as an electron acceptor. Sulfur respiration can cause hydrogen sulfide to be produced, which is highly toxic to tree roots. Sulfur respiration also causes many compounds to bond with sulfides, making them insoluble and unusable.

Fermentation comes at the end of the respiration process that lacks oxygen. Fermentation is the transfer of electrons to carbon. Compared to normal respiration, fermentation respiration consumes 20 times the amount of food for the same amount of energy produced (Table 1). Various hydrocarbons, alcohols, fatty acids, phenolic acids, sulfur compounds, and cyanogenic compounds are produced. Also generated are methane, carbon dioxide, hydrogen, and nitrogen gas. These materials escape as gas bubbles, dissolve in the water, or float

to the water surface. Many of these materials are toxic to tree roots and stem tissues in moderate concentrations. Flood-tolerant tree species have developed some mechanisms for expelling, storing, or disassembling these byproducts in small amounts.

Under fermentation conditions, root cells quickly use all their carbohydrate stores. Because the root cells are made of carbon compounds, microbes begin consuming them. The result of fermentation is an electron-rich solution with no place to transfer electrons in order to generate energy. Sulfur and fermentation respiration produce a stinky, slimy soup of materials. Trees will not survive long under these conditions.

Tree and Soil Health

Through the progressive stages of respiration without oxygen, roots are badly stressed. Final root death is a combination of suffocation, starvation, and increased concentrations of toxic chemicals. Organisms in the environment that can perform anaerobic (without oxygen) respiration continue to consume the carbon materials of the roots.

Many floodwaters carry large amounts of organic materials derived from sewage, agricultural areas, and organic soil layers. These waterborne organic materials act as a food source for many microorganisms that require oxygen. Large organic loads in floodwaters cause the quick use of any available oxygen dissolved in the water.

Flooding in the growing season is worse for trees than dormant-season flooding.

Soil structure can be directly damaged by excessive water. Soil aggregates fall apart from reduced cohesion, dissolved metallic and organic coatings, and dispersed clay particles. The weight of soil and water and the effect of any activities on the top of flooded soil can crush and destroy structural units. In addition, water leaches and disrupts many essential elements held in the soil and organic materials.

Decomposition

The breakdown or decomposition of organic matter in normal soils helps hold tree-essential cations and anions, releases essential elements, and prevents leaching of elements. This decomposition process is composed of many organisms under aerobic conditions. In normal soils, decomposition of organic matter yields carbon dioxide and humus. Carbon dioxide moves into the atmosphere, and components of the humus are bound to clays and oxides of aluminum and iron. This binding process improves soil structure. The nitrogen in the soil that is released as ammonia is converted to nitrate. Sulfur compounds are oxidized to sulfates.

In flooded soils, the decomposition of organic matter is by anaerobic bacteria and occurs at less than half the rate of aerobic decomposition. These organisms are less diverse and much more inefficient at decomposition than aerobes. Soil structure can be disrupted. Nitrogen and sulfur are lost or are combined in unusable or toxic forms. Slick, slimy layers of partially decayed organic matter remain.

Tree Parts and Problems

Flooding affects trees at every stage of their development, from seed germination, flowering, sprouting, and elongation growth. At each life stage, flooding can cause injury, changes in anatomy and growth form, decline, and death.

Leaf and Shoot Problems

Within hours of flooding, photosynthesis is shut down. Photosynthesis is limited over increasing time periods by the loss of carbon

Probably the most limiting and immediate aspect of flooding on trees is the lack of oxygen.

fixation enzymes, loss of chlorophyll, reduction of leaf area, and leaf abscission. Photosynthesis is an expensive system to maintain and very sensitive to internal and external environmental changes. Once flooding is over, it takes an extended time (months/seasons) for photosynthetic activities to return to normal.

Another significant problem is the slowing of transpiration. Transpiration is primarily a physical process driven by atmospheric relative humidity with biological control valves. There are several places along the transpiration stream that indirect energy input by the tree is required. Energy for maintaining cell functions, stomates, and pressure adjustments is quickly compromised under flooded conditions. The ironic result is the drying of tree parts above water while the tree is surrounded with water. Water loss continues during flooded conditions, while uptake declines greatly in the roots.

Flooding initiates many growth regulator problems. Growth regulators are how one part of a tree communicates with other parts. The messages are carried by different types of chemicals. The production of these growth regulation chemicals (and their destruction once the message is delivered) is affected by oxygen levels and tree health. Auxin, ethylene, and abscisic acid concentrations increase in flooded trees, while gibberellic acids and cytokinins decrease. The correlated result is leaf epinasty, senescence and abscission, stem growth disruption, and adventitious root production.

Flooding changes the ecology of the soil, causing anaerobic organisms to replace aerobic organisms. Anaerobic conditions initiate several symptoms that include no growth, poor leaf expansion, limited leaf formation, leaf yellowing, premature senescence and fall color formation, and leaf drop (with older leaves falling first). Leaf drop can take from two weeks in upland species to eight weeks in wetland species after flooding. Wetland species can be damaged just as badly as upland species by warm, growing-season floods.

Root Problems

Flooding causes a loss of the extent, reach, and health of tree roots. Noticeable root growth loss occurs within seven days. For active growth, roots must have a soil atmosphere with at least 5 percent oxygen. Over time, decline, death, and decay are the results of flooding. Generally under flooded conditions, woody roots survive and nonwoody roots die. Fungi (such as *Phytophthora* or *Pythium*) that tolerate low soil oxygen attack these stressed tree roots. Loss of roots makes the tree prone to drought damage and windthrow across the next several years. Some of these problems may not become apparent for two or three years.

Root problems include poor uptake of essential elements and additional resource loss through leakage from root membranes. Nitrogen is lost in the soil and throughout the tree under flooded conditions. Nitrate in the soil is lost by denitrification to atmospheric nitrogen and through production of nitrogen oxides. At the same time, the roots are not taking up available nitrogen because of organic acid shortages from the leaves and from lack of food.

Flooding also suppresses mycorrhizal fungi, which are strongly aerobic. Poor phosphorus and potassium uptake is an associated problem. Other oxygen-requiring organisms in the soil surrounding the roots are killed. These organisms normally help recycle elements for trees. The tree can develop many nutritional problems after floods.

Air Space Problems

The tree aerates as much of its tissues as possible. Oxygen is available through lenticel and stomate openings and can move for short distances in both wood and bark. Flooded trees produce larger, more open lenticels that are connected to intercellular spaces and can provide more oxygen transport. Some trees use vertical air roots to assist with oxygenation. Modified roots such as cypress knees (*Taxodium* spp.) do not effectively transport oxygen but act as structural supports for anchoring the root system.

One growth response of trees to flooding is production of proportionally greater numbers of thin-walled cells called parenchyma. This cell type is found in both the xylem and phloem. Resin duct numbers also are increased in species with these features. Flooding initiates production of low-density cells and more intercellular spaces in the xylem, phloem, and bark to facilitate oxygen transport and removal of toxic materials.

Anatomical Changes

Trees can generate a tissue called aerenchyma, which is made of thin-walled cells with large intercellular spaces. This tissue forms by cells dissolving and cell walls separating to form a spongy mass of cells with large air spaces. Loblolly pine (*Pinus taeda*) is one species capable of producing aerenchyma.

Most trees immediately slow or stop growth under flooded conditions. Old myths suggest trees grow larger in diameter when flooded. A diameter

Individual trees, including those within the same species, may respond differently to flooding.

PHOTO CREDIT: JEFFREY ILES.

increase can occur in some species and is caused by bark and wood tissues producing more spaces between cells and producing larger cells with thinner walls. This low-density tree tissue around the outside of a tree can represent a large-diameter growth spurt. In some trees, this growth pattern may be a prelude to final rapid decline and death.

Flooding also can initiate many adventitious roots on the submerged stem area and large roots. The more flood-tolerant the species, the more likely the species will form adventitious roots. Adventitious roots increase the capacity of the tree to uptake materials, oxygenate the rhizosphere, detoxify soil materials, and increase root growth regulators.

Seedling Problems

Flood tolerance of seedlings and young trees varies greatly by species and can be different than that of mature trees of the same species. Coverage of foliage with water is a critical feature in initiating flood damage—the longer the leaves are under water, the more damage. Young trees also can be buried by sediment, pushed over, or swept away. Major damage can occur along the young stem and root collar area that may haunt the tree throughout the rest of its life.

Problems Caused by Siltation and Erosion

One of the most important long-term, flood-related growth problems affecting a tree is siltation, or sediment deposition. Soil fill deposited over the root system can range from a few fine particles to 6 feet (or more) of various-textured sediments. Soil fill requires a quick root response to new soil conditions. Trees under these conditions generate a new root system in new locations. Some species are not effective in reacting to these kinds of changes in a timely manner and will decline and die.

Another significant long-term problem

Decline and death as a result of prolonged flooding.

PHOTO CREDIT: JOHN LLOYD.

is soil erosion. Some trees will be left without soil covering their roots, or the trees may not have enough soil around and under the roots to keep them structurally stable. Addition of small amounts of soil fill, composted organic matter, and mulch can help prevent roots from drying in the sun.

Tree Toppling

One aspect of flood damage, especially after flash- or scouring-flood conditions, is the toppling of trees. Trees stand erect against most wind and flood conditions. Trees tend to sway back and forth in the wind as they are loaded and unloaded. The period of the sway is set by mechanical properties of the tree and soil. Swaying can loosen tree roots from wet soil and lead to toppling under light winds. When a tree is partially under water in a moving flow, there is more constant pressure on the tree and less swaying.

The primary strategies for resisting flood waters in trees are stiffness, deformation to reduce drag, and stem and root strength. A tree stands because its stiff, heavy, wide-based trunk provides mass and a center of gravity that moves little laterally. As more of the stem and crown become inundated, more drag is generated by stems, twigs, and foliage. The force generated on the tree by flowing water is at least 3.5 times the force generated by wind at the same velocity. Additionally, as one tree falls over, the force of falling puts additional stress on

downstream neighboring trees. A domino effect of tree toppling may occur.

Flowing Water Problems

The flow of floodwaters carries solid materials that can abrade and injure trees. The force of the moving water propels floating materials, rolls or moves solid items along the bottom of the flow, or suspends materials. Small particles can act as sandpaper, tearing at the bark. Larger items, such as ice, lumber, and other trees, can run into standing trees and produce injuries up and down the stem depending on water height. Wave actions can injure stem and root crown areas.

Flood flow can bring a wide range of chemicals and dissolved solids to the tree and its soil resources. Simple sediment deposition is made more damaging by organic and chemical loads from upstream. Although most materials are extremely diluted, some materials in the water can have long-lasting effects. Floods of mixed industrial areas can bring many things downstream and in contact with trees and soil resources. Biological and chemical hazards may be present in floodwater and can injure trees and cleanup crews.

Eroding Root-Holds

Flood flows can erode the soils holding roots in place and supporting the weight of the tree. Removal of soil from around roots that mechanically hold the tree erect under tension will reduce root–soil friction, reduce soil strength, and allow for increased movement of roots and the tree. Removal of soil from around basal roots that are holding the tree erect under compression will increase the probability for root bending, shearing, and fracturing, and tree toppling.

Standing trees generate intense vortexes in flowing water that can remove large amounts of soil from around the stem base and from around large roots. Erosion can make the

Table 2. Flood tolerance of selected trees. Different flood conditions, unique site situations, and individual trees from various parts of a species' range will all have different responses to flooded conditions. This table presents a general summary for illustrative purposes.

INTOLERANT OF FLOODING

sugar maple	*Acer saccharum*	white pine	*Pinus strobus*
yellow buckeye	*Aesculus flava*	shortleaf pine	*Pinus echinata*
shagbark hickory	*Carya ovata*	black cherry	*Prunus serotina*
mockernut hickory	*Carya tomentosa*	Callery pear	*Pyrus* spp.
Eastern redbud	*Cercis canadensis*	white oak	*Quercus alba*
dogwood	*Cornus florida*	southern red oak	*Quercus falcata*
American beech	*Fagus grandifolia*	blackjack oak	*Quercus marilandica*
American ash	*Fraxinus americana*	chinkapin oak	*Quercus muehlenbergii*
black walnut	*Juglans nigra*	post oak	*Quercus stellata*
Eastern redcedar	*Juniperus virginiana*	black locust	*Robinia pseudoacacia*
tulip poplar	*Liriodendron tulipifera*	sassafras	*Sassafras albidum*
sourwood	*Oxydendrum arboreum*	basswood	*Tilia americana*
Virginia pine	*Pinus virginiana*		

TOLERANT OF FLOODING

boxelder	*Acer negundo*	waxmyrtle	*Myrica cerifera*
red maple	*Acer rubra*	Ogeechee lime	*Nyssa ogeche*
silver maple	*Acer saccharinum*	black gum	*Nyssa sylvatica*
Ohio buckeye	*Aesculus glabra*	redbay	*Persea borbonia*
red buckeye	*Aesculus pavia*	spruce pine	*Pinus glabra*
alder	*Alnus glutinosa*	water elm	*Planera aquatica*
devil's walkingstick	*Aralia spinosa*	sycamore	*Platanus occidentalis*
river birch	*Betula nigra*	cottonwood	*Populus deltoides*
pecan	*Carya illinoensis*	swamp white oak	*Quercus bicolor*
water hickory	*Carya aquatica*	overcup oak	*Quercus lyrata*
sugarberry	*Celtis laevigata*	bur oak	*Quercus macrocarpa*
hackberry	*Celtis occidentalis*	water oak	*Quercus nigra*
hawthorn	*Crataegus* spp.	Nuttall oak	*Quercus nuttallii*
persimmon	*Diospyros virginiana*	pin oak	*Quercus palustris*
green ash	*Fraxinus pennsylvanica*	willow	*Salix* spp.
honeylocust	*Gleditsia triacanthos*	elder	*Sambucus* spp.
dahoon holly	*Ilex cassine*	redwood	*Sequoia sempervirens*
possumhaw	*Ilex decidua*	pondcypress	*Taxodium ascendens*
sweetgum	*Liquidambar styraciflua*	baldcypress	*Taxodium distichum*
sweetbay	*Magnolia virginiana*	white-cedar	*Thuja occidentalis*
osage-orange	*Maclura pomifera*	winged elm	*Ulmus alata*
dawn redwood	*Metasequoia glyptostroboides*	American elm	*Ulmus americana*

tree much more susceptible to wind and water pressure failures. Erosion also can lead to tree structural failure after flooding when normal moisture conditions have been regained.

Structurally unstable trees can be at great risk for unexpected collapse. Flood cleanup operations can be endangered from damaged trees, as can people and property around the structurally damaged tree. The risks associated with structural problems can be compounded by other types of damage, by time, and by other site changes. Several years may be needed to fully determine the extent of flood damage to trees and any increased liability risks.

Flood Tolerance

The role of a tree under flooded conditions is to maintain growth regulator connections and food supply to all cells it can and to avoid accumulating toxins. Trees can generally be rated on a gradient ranging from flood intolerant to flood tolerant. A number of growth form, anatomical, and physiological changes available in tolerant plants attempt to minimize flooding damage and growth constraints. Table 2 provides a list of selected example species.

Flood Timing

Flooding in the growing season is worse for trees than dormant-season flooding, especially if the air temperature is warm. The higher the temperature, the faster and more severely any oxygen shortage will be felt, and the more the top of a tree will dehydrate. Flooding during warm, growing-season periods magnifies flood damage because of respiration needs, water oxygen contents, and foliage water loss (Table 1).

Floodwater quality is critical. Stagnant water usually is more damaging than flowing water. Flowing water can carry debris that physically damages trees. Flowing water does have turbulent mixing that moves oxygen more effectively to root surfaces than standing water.

As general rules:

- broad-leaved trees [including baldcypress (*Taxodium* spp.)] tolerate flooding better than conifer species
- middle-aged trees tolerate flooding better than young and old trees
- dormant-season flooding with cold air and water temperatures is the least damaging to trees
- floods during the spring startup period (varies by species phenology) and the fall senescence period are the most damaging to trees

• foliage covered by floodwater is extremely damaging to the tree

Best Management Practices for Flood Damage

Activities that can be done immediately, or by the end of the current growing season, to mitigate flood damage to trees:

- First, perform an assessment of tree survival, structural risks, and health conditions.
- Prevent foot and vehicular traffic over the site (tree rooting area) until water levels and soil saturation have fallen to a level at which any more compaction and rutting will not occur.
- Drain excess water from the site as soon as possible without causing more root damage.
- Immediately cover exposed tree roots with a thin layer of soil, composted organic matter, and mulch.
- Remove deposited sediments quickly and carefully without further damaging roots.
- Prevent further soil erosion.
- Correct and modify site drainage patterns.
- Begin aeration and structural improvements to soils.
- Use soil testing to determine proper essential element management once soil is back to "normal."
- You may need to add phosphorus, potassium, calcium, and magnesium. These applications, if needed, should be repeated over several seasons to correct and enrich soil resource values for tree growth. Use soil testing often because soils "normalize."
- Add one light dose of nitrogen, approximately 0.5 pounds of nitrogen per 1,000 square feet of open soil surface area, within the past drip line area of the tree after the site has returned to normal moisture content. After this application, do not fertilize with nitrogen again until after full leaf expansion in the following growing season. In each of the next three years, apply 1 pound of nitrogen per 1,000 square feet of open soil surface area over the season to correct and enrich soil

resource values and to reorganize nitrogen cycling in the tree and soil. Do not overdose areas with nitrogen.
- You may add very small amounts of calcium sulfate to return sulfur to the soil, if required.

Other guidelines:

- Do not add microelements.
- Do as little green-wood pruning as possible to conserve tree food supplies. Minimize wounding, especially wounds that present heartwood exposure.
- Prune trees for safety concerns and risk reduction.
- Beware of pathogenic and insect attacks on stressed trees and make appropriate responses where needed. Both the trees under attack and surrounding trees may require therapeutic or preventive treatments.
- Many items will have washed downstream in the flood. Most materials will have been extremely diluted. Be cautious with activities in flood damaged areas. Dust, soil, water, animals, and chemicals provide hazards. Always wash thoroughly after activities in the flood-damaged areas.
- In your cleanup activities, do not change land-use types or perform large-scale soil movement and major water channelization/drainage without contacting your local USDA-Natural Resource Conservation Service.
- You may need to amend soils with microbial and composted organic materials.
- Carefully monitor soil moisture contents and be prepared to add supplemental water to trees. Newly developed roots in new locations can be quickly damaged by "normal" conditions.
- Add structural supports to valuable trees at risk of structural failure, where applicable.
- Upright partially tipped, valuable trees if more than 50 percent of the roots remain. These trees will need permanent guying.
- Install a proper tree care and maintenance program that incorporates plant health care (PHC) principles.

- Safely remove, with minimum site damage, trees that are hazardous, dead, or not meeting new management objectives for the flood-damaged site.

Over the long run, tree vigor and structural stability will remain a concern. Pest problems, because of the massive number of stressed trees in the area, will reach peak populations quickly and present a management problem for as many as five years into the future. Flooded soil conditions can quickly turn healthy trees into declining, pest-attacked trees. If the tree was healthy and structurally sound before the flood and resulting oxygen shortage, it has a good chance at recovery over the next few years.

Kim Coder is a professor in the School of Forest Resources at the University of Georgia, Athens, Georgia.

TEST QUESTIONS

To receive continuing education unit (CEU) credit (1 CEU) for home study of this article, after you have read it, darken the appropriate circles on the answer form in the back of this book. **Be sure to use the answer form that corresponds to this article.** Each question has only one correct answer. A passing score for this test is 80 percent. Photocopies of the answer form are **not** acceptable.

After you have answered the questions on the answer form, complete the registration information on the form and send it to ISA, P.O. Box 3129, Champaign, IL 61826-3129.

You will be notified only if you do not pass. CEU codes for the exams you have passed will appear on your CEU updates. If you do not pass, you have the option of taking the test as often as necessary.

1. Floods disrupt soil biology and root growth by
   a. destroying soil texture
   b. limiting oxygen availability
   c. rinsing away excess carbon dioxide (CO_2)
   d. washing away structural roots

2. When oxygen is no longer available in the soil for microbe respiration,
   a. aerobic bacteria will thrive
   b. nitrogen will be used
   c. photosynthesis will accelerate
   d. all of the above

3. Decomposition of organic matter in soils under flooded conditions
   a. can generate many materials toxic to trees
   b. generates methane, nitrogen, and hydrogen gas bubbles
   c. is at least 50 percent slower than normal
   d. all of the above

4. Flowing floodwaters can
   a. keep trees upright because of the weight of the water
   b. initiate more dense bark growth
   c. concentrate fermentation products
   d. injure trees with carried debris

5. An attribute not directly affecting the destructiveness of a flood on trees is
   a. temperature
   b. water depth
   c. tree rooting depth
   d. water oxygen content

6. Oxygen in respiration processes is considered to be
   a. electron-dense
   b. electron-hungry
   c. inert
   d. an electron donor

7. The microbial populations in a warm soil can use all available oxygen within
   a. minutes of flooding
   b. hours of flooding
   c. days of flooding
   d. weeks of flooding

8. When floodwaters are carrying large volumes of organic materials,
   a. cation exchange values will be increased in the soil
   b. little oxygen will be available in the water
   c. microorganism numbers will fall
   d. the additional nutrients will initiate tree growth

9. Oxygen reaches the roots most effectively through
   a. diffusion through warm water
   b. lenticels in the soil
   c. macropores in the soil
   d. micropores in the soil

10. The first noticeable process in a tree to be stopped by flooding is
    a. abscission
    b. respiration
    c. photosynthesis
    d. transpiration

11. As soil oxygen contents fall below five percent,
    a. fermentation begins
    b. root growth stops
    c. soil organic matter stops decaying
    d. soil structure begins to fall apart

12. New tissues generated after flooding can have
    a. greater number of extractives
    b. larger stomates
    c. thicker cell walls
    d. wider intercellular spaces

13. A tree that is listed as flood tolerant
    a. can be killed by flood damage
    b. may not be able to adjust to changing flood conditions
    c. will be most likely to survive flooding
    d. all of the above

14. A major concern with younger or shorter trees and floodwater is
    a. fermentation of the buds and twigs
    b. increased cytokinins in tissues.
    c. loss of calcium and magnesium
    d. water covering the foliage

15. One of the essential elements made much more mobile and toxic by flooding is
    a. carbon (C)
    b. calcium (Ca)
    c. manganese (Mn)
    d. potassium (K)

16. Floodwaters normally contain significant amounts of
    a. human disease organisms
    b. petrochemical products.
    c. sewage from humans and animals
    d. all of the above

17. In general, for every 18°F temperature increase above 40°F,
    a. fewer aerenchyma cells are generated
    b. fermentation rates increase in the soil by 80 percent
    c. respiration rates in the soil and in roots double
    d. respiration rates fall by one-half

18. The most survivable flood for trees occurs
    a. after full leaf expansion in summer
    b. during a cool, dormant season
    c. during a hot, dormant season
    d. once fall senescence has begun

19. The first action to be taken after floodwaters have receded is to
    a. assess tree survival, structural risks, and health
    b. immediately add a complete, high-nitrogen fertilizer
    c. remove all damaged trees from the site
    d. use pesticides to prevent attacks

20. A major problem with fast-flowing floodwaters and trees is
    a. decline in water storage in heartwood
    b. dilution of essential elements available to trees
    c. erosion around the tree base and major roots
    d. excessive oxygen delivery to stem tissues

ANALYZE BEFORE YOU FERTILIZE

By E. Thomas Smiley

This article originally appeared in Arbor Age *magazine, Volume 14, Issue 4 (1994).*

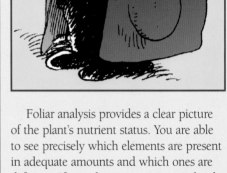

Learning objectives—
The arborist will be able to

- describe the correct procedures for collecting samples for foliar and soil analysis.
- explain why nutrient problems should be diagnosed before undertaking a program of fertilization.
- discuss the potential limitations of foliar analysis.

In the past, most arborists, when asked to fertilize trees or shrubs, would mix up a batch of their favorite fertilizer brew and inject an unknown amount deep into the soil and hope for a positive response. That approach shows a general lack of understanding about tree and shrub fertilization. Dealing with the wide variety of elements that can make up part of a fertilizer, along with different needs and responses of trees and shrubs and different soil types, adds to the confusion.

With concerns about the role of fertilizers in groundwater contamination, fertilizer runoff, overfertilization, and fertilizer burn, the knowledgeable arborist needs to accurately diagnose nutrient problems and target fertilizer applications to correct them.

It is impossible to cover all aspects of fertilizer in one article, so we will concentrate on diagnosis of nutrient problems. As with insect and disease problems, you need to identify the exact cause before you can treat it. You would never treat Diplodia tip blight with an insecticide, so why would you treat a manganese deficiency with nitrogen? But that is exactly what many arborists do.

Diagnoses can be made visually or by using a nutrient analysis. Visual diagnoses are made by examining leaf color, leaf size, pattern of discoloration, and twig growth rates. With experience, the visual method provides the correct diagnosis of severe deficiencies most of the time. But what about mild deficiencies? Many plants in urban areas are less productive than they could be because of mild deficiencies, often referred to as "hidden hunger." Hidden hunger may predispose plants to winter injury and drought damage and may impede natural defenses against some insect and disease pests.

FOLIAR ANALYSIS

To get a true picture of the nutrient status in a tree or shrub, you should perform a foliar nutrient status analysis. This test entails collecting mature leaves that are exposed to full sun. Fill a paper lunch bag half full of leaves and ship them to a diagnostic laboratory the same day. The laboratory will dry the leaves, grind them into a powder, and extract the nutrient elements, then analyze the extract by using a spectrometer to determine the quantity of each nutrient element. An analysis report containing nutrient concentrations and a high, medium, or low nutrient rating will be sent to you.

Foliar analysis provides a clear picture of the plant's nutrient status. You are able to see precisely which elements are present in adequate amounts and which ones are deficient. If any elements are at toxic levels, that should be noted.

Using this information, you will be able to tailor your fertilizer program to correct the specific nutrient deficiency while avoiding the cost and possible environmental concerns from applying large quantities of unnecessary elements.

While foliar analysis sounds like a panacea, you may encounter a few problems. First is the cost of analysis. State laboratories, which usually are associated with land grant university soil science departments, can cost five to fifteen dollars per sample. With a private laboratory, costs may range from fifteen to thirty dollars. Laboratories may charge additional to test for certain elements.

Another problem with foliar analysis is the lack of standard foliar nutrient values for healthy plants. While these values are easily found for virtually all agricultural crops, including pine and fruit trees, they are difficult to find for ornamental species. Without this baseline, it is difficult to determine if the trees or shrubs are at the hidden-hunger nutrient level.

One way to compensate for the lack of standard values is to submit more than one foliar sample. In addition to sending in the sample from the problem tree, also send in samples from a tree you know is healthy. Comparing the data will provide insight into deficiencies.

Foliar analysis identifies which nutrients are at less-than-desirable levels, but that does not necessarily mean that they are deficient in the soil. For example, when manganese is deficient in the leaves, there often is a soil pH problem that is restricting manganese uptake. Adding manganese fertilizer to the soil without correcting the pH may be of little benefit.

Soil Analysis

Analyzing the soil in addition to or instead of the foliage can provide information needed for fertilization. Soil analysis is less expensive than foliar analysis and provides data on soil pH, organic-matter levels, and cation exchange capacity. This information may be reflected in foliar analysis, but direct soil analysis can aid in assessing these soil characteristics.

Most laboratories that analyze soil provide bags or boxes for sample submission. You should have a supply of these containers as well as sample submission forms.

Collect soil samples within the drip line of trees or shrubs to a depth of 6 inches. Use a soil-sampling tube, trowel, or shovel to collect four to ten samples. Mix the samples together in a clean plastic bucket, remove any rocks, mulch, and plugs of turf, then transfer the required amount of soil, usually 2 cups, to the laboratory container.

When your sample arrives at the testing lab, they will dry it and grind it, then extract the nutrients in a solution and run them through a spectrometer to determine nutrient levels.

Soil pH is analyzed in the laboratory the same way it is measured in the field using a pocket pH meter. Soil is mixed with an equal volume of distilled water, and a pH probe is placed in the solution until the reading becomes constant. While the laboratory uses a more sophisticated pH meter,

the answer usually will be within 0.2 of a reading taken with a quality pocket pH meter.

Like a foliar analysis report, the soil analysis report provides information on nutrient levels, usually expressed in parts per million or pounds per acre. Along with this information will be high, medium, and low ratings and recommendations. If maximum plant health is the goal of your fertilization program, any nutrient in the medium or low category should be applied in the fertilization. Optimal soil pH varies with plant species. Some prefer acid soil; others prefer neutral or alkaline soils. You will need to consult a table of optimal pH levels by species before undertaking pH modifications. These tables usually are available from your local Extension office.

Most hardwood species grow best in soils with organic-matter levels greater than three percent. If soil tests below that level, consider organic amendments.

Cation exchange capacity (CEC) is a measurement of the soil's ability to retain many plant nutrients. It is dependent on soil texture, especially type and amount of clay and organic matter. For soils with very low CEC levels, addition of organic amendments may be beneficial. In addition, because low CEC soil does not retain nutrients well, more frequent light fertilizer applications may be required.

Like diagnosing pest problems before treating them, accurate diagnosis of nutrient problems should be done before fertilization. The benefits to the plant and to the environment are numerous. The first step in this direction is to begin collecting samples for analysis, then modifying your fertilizer and soil amendment practices to address specific deficiencies.

Tom Smiley is an arboricultural researcher at the Bartlett Tree Research Laboratories and adjunct professor at Clemson University.

1. Visual diagnoses are made by examining
   a. leaf color
   b. leaf size
   c. twig growth rates
   d. all of the above

2. "Hidden hunger" is not a problem to plants in urban areas.
   a. true
   b. false

3. Potential limitations associated with foliar analysis include all of the following **except**:
   a. it does not include information on nutrient levels in the soil
   b. the cost of analysis
   c. a lack of standard foliar nutrient values
   d. accuracy

4. Optimal soil pH levels for plants
   a. are always in the alkaline range
   b. vary with plant species
   c. are the same with all plant species
   d. are always in the acid range

5. The best way to gather leaves for a foliar analysis is to
   a. dry the leaves first before shipping
   b. carefully place one leaf in a sterile container
   c. collect the most juvenile leaves
   d. fill a paper lunch bag half full of leaves

6. Soil samples should be collected 4 to 6 feet outside the drip line.
   a. true
   b. false

7. If maximum plant health is the goal of your fertilization program, only nutrients in the low category should be applied in the fertilization.
   a. true
   b. false

8. Cation exchange capacity is dependent on
   a. soil texture and organic matter
   b. amount of roots in the soil
   c. soil structure
   d. soil water percolation rates

9. Soil analysis provides information on
   a. soil pH
   b. organic-matter levels
   c. cation exchange capacity
   d. all of the above

10. Accurate diagnosis of nutrient problems should be done
    a. before fertilization
    b. after fertilization
    c. either before or after fertilization
    d. none of the above

FERTILIZING TREES AND SHRUBS

PART 1 Determining If, When, and What to Use

By E. Thomas Smiley, Sharon Lilly, and Patrick Kelsey

Trees require certain essential elements or "nutrients" to function and grow. A nutrient is an element involved in the metabolism of a tree or necessary for a tree to complete its life cycle. For trees growing on a forest site, these elements normally are present in sufficient quantities in the soil. Landscape trees or urban trees, however, may be growing in soils that do not contain sufficient available elements for satisfactory growth and development. Topsoil often is removed during construction. Leaves and other plant parts are removed in landscape maintenance, disrupting nutrient cycling and the return of organic matter to the soil. It may be necessary to fertilize or to adjust soil pH to increase nutrient availability.

Fertilizing a tree can increase growth and can, under certain circumstances, help reverse declining health (Figure 1). However, if the fertilizer is not needed or not applied correctly, it may not benefit the tree at all. In fact, it may increase susceptibility to certain pests and accelerate decline. Trees with satisfactory growth and not showing symptoms of nutrient deficiency may not require fertilization. Trees growing in turf that is heavily fertilized may not require additional fertilization. It is important to recognize when a tree needs fertilization, which elements are needed, and when and how they should be applied.

Why Fertilize Trees?

Trees require certain elements, known as macronutrients, in relatively large quantities. The

> ### Learning objectives—
> ### The arborist will be able to
>
> - discuss the potential advantages and limitations of fertilizing trees in the landscape.
> - explain the importance of basing fertilization on prescription and discuss the limitations of soil and foliar analyses.
> - describe the different types of fertilizer available and when the use of various types might be appropriate.
> - discuss how soil pH should influence the choice of fertilizer.

most important of these macronutrients is nitrogen (N). Nitrogen is a constituent of proteins and chlorophyll, and it is critical to photosynthesis and other plant processes.

Under natural conditions, nitrogen comes largely from organic matter in the soil. Soil organisms decompose organic matter, releasing nitrate ions (NO_3^-) and ammonium ions (NH_4^+), which, in turn, can be further converted to nitrate ions. The positively charged ammonium ions are adsorbed to soil particles (clay), while the negatively charged nitrate ions are free in the soil water to be picked up by plant roots or leached down through the soil. Much of the nitrogen in soil is lost due to leaching or to volatilization (the return of nitrogen to the atmosphere in its gaseous state). The removal of leaf litter and other natural sources of nitrogen can disrupt the cycling of nitrogen in the soil.

Nitrogen deficiency shows up as slow growth, small leaves, and yellowing (chlorosis) of the leaves, especially the older leaves. On nitrogen-deficient plants, sometimes the newer, developing leaves appear greener than the older leaves because nitrogen is somewhat mobile within plants, allowing it to be directed toward new growth. However, these symptoms also could be the result of a variety of other problems that affect root health and element uptake. Because nitrogen is the element most likely to be deficient in trees, fertilizer specifications usually focus on this element.

In addition to nitrogen, the elements phosphorus (P), potassium (K), and sulfur (S) also are required in relatively large quantities. These elements often are present in the soil in adequate amounts for trees and large shrubs. The secondary nutrients include magnesium (Mg) and calcium (Ca) and are required in

Figure 1. If a tree is lacking essential elements, fertilization can improve health, growth, and appearance. The trees on the left were fertilized; the trees on the right were not.

moderate quantities. Although these elements are called secondary, severe deficiencies can result in loss of the plant. Magnesium deficiency is a serious problem in palms.

Other elements, known as micronutrients, are required in lesser quantities. Although these elements are not required in large amounts, a deficiency of any one can have profound effects on the health of the tree. For example, iron chlorosis is a condition that results when a tree is not absorbing sufficient quantities of iron, usually due to a high soil pH. The young leaves are small and chlorotic (yellow), often with green veins, while the older leaves tend to be darker green. Iron deficiency can eventually kill a tree. Like iron, manganese and zinc may at times be deficient in a tree. The remaining elements—molybdenum, copper, chlorine, boron, and nickel—are less likely to be deficient. Soil pH has a major influence on micronutrient availability.

Determing Goals and Objectives

The goal of fertilization is to supply nutrients determined to be deficient to achieve a clearly defined objective.

Common objectives of fertilization include to

- overcome a visible nutrient deficiency
- eliminate a deficiency not obviously visible that was detected through soil or foliar analysis
- increase vegetative growth, flowering, or fruiting
- increase the vitality of the plant

When Not to Fertilize

Certain factors should be considered before fertilization. Fertilizer may not be necessary or beneficial when trees or shrubs have

- sufficient levels of all essential elements so that growth rate and condition of health are acceptable to the landscape manager
- potential for certain pest problems that may be exacerbated by fertilization
- herbicide damage with residual activity in the plant

Some pest problems are increased with fertilization. Nutrients can promote the population of the pest or reduce resistance

within the tree. Several plant–pest combinations have been well studied. Examples of some of the potential interactions are presented in Table 1. If a plant requires fertilization and has one or more of the pests that are promoted by fertilization, application should be made in conjunction with pest treatment or after the pest population has been reduced. In such cases, apply fertilizer after soil or foliar nutrient analysis has confirmed the deficiency and has been used to prescribe the treatment.

Table 1. Pests promoted or plant resistance decreased by fertilization.

Spider Mites

Insects
  aphids
  adelgids
  psyllids
  scale
  whiteflies
  lacebug
  some caterpillars

Diseases
  pine pitch canker
  fire blight

Abiotic
  herbicides

Soil Testing and Plant Analysis

The most accurate way to determine a tree's nutrient needs is to obtain laboratory analyses of the soil and leaves (Figure 2). To determine the need for fertilization, you should consider obtaining three analyses:

- foliar nutrient analysis to determine the nutrient content of the leaves
- soil nutrient analysis to determine soil nutrient levels and salt content
- pH analysis to determine the acidity or alkalinity of the soil

Foliar nutrient analysis is used to determine the current nutrient content of leaves. Results provide information

on which nutrients have been absorbed and translocated within the plant. This method is the most accurate for determining deficiencies of most elements. However, it does not provide information on why the nutrients are deficient. Foliar nutrient analysis usually is more expensive than soil analysis.

A soil analysis can give information about the presence of essential elements, soil pH, organic matter, and cation exchange capacity (Figure 3). The pH and salt content (especially in arid regions) are important for recommending treatments and selecting fertilizers. Matching the fertilizer nutrient content to the deficient elements ensures that the proper nutrients are applied to correct the deficiency. Adding only the elements required means that excess elements will not be introduced into the environment. The process of conducting analyses, setting plant health goals, and selecting a fertilizer to achieve the goal is called "prescription fertilization."

Nitrogen is the most commonly deficient nutrient for landscape plants. It also is one of the most difficult to measure in a soil analysis because of the numerous forms that nitrogen can take in the soil (for example, nitrate, ammonium, or urea). Nitrogen also is rapidly transformed among forms. Even under ideal sampling and testing conditions, the analyses often do not correlate well with plant response to fertilization. Because the correlation between soil analysis levels and plant response to fertilizer is not always good, nitrogen recommendations

Figure 2. Laboratory analysis can provide diagnostic information about nutrient presence in the soil or foilage. Interpretation of laboratory results is still an important part of the diagnosis and subsequent treatment recommendations.

Figure 3. Sample soil analysis report.

also should be based on foliar nutrient analysis, visual assessment of the plant, and the fertilization objective.

Phosphorus (P), potassium (K), magnesium (Mg), and calcium (Ca) levels are determined using one of several methods of soil extraction. Caution is in order because various laboratories use different extraction methods; therefore, direct comparison of numbers among laboratories may be difficult. Although interpretation is a nonexact science, analysis results correlate to the probability of plant response to fertilizer treatment with the element. For example, if the analysis for a given element is "very low," there is a high probability of plant response to fertilization with that element. Conversely, if the analysis is "high," there is a low probability of response to treatment.

Soil tests also should give an analysis of the organic matter (OM) in the soil. If high levels of organic matter are present, there usually will be high levels of beneficial soil microorganisms and nutrients available to the plant. The reported level is a percentage of the weight of the soil. Levels of 3 percent or more are preferable for most plants; higher levels are beneficial for macro-nutrient availability.

The cation exchange capacity (CEC) of the soil is one measure of the soil's ability to retain certain elements. When CEC values are low, more frequent fertilization may be required, and the risk of leaching is higher. When the CEC is high, applications should be required less frequently, and the risk of leaching is lower.

When you select a fertilizer for a specific area or site, the fertilizer choice may be affected by the pH of the soil. When fertilizing a site that is too alkaline for the plant, choosing an acidic fertilizer may reduce the need for direct pH adjustment and may allow the fertilizer to be more effective.

When taking a soil sample, take six to ten cores from representative locations of the entire area or root zone. Typical sampling depth is to 6 inches—the location of the majority of fine roots (Figure 4). These cores should be mixed together in a clean, nonmetallic container or soil sample bag. This procedure will give results that are averaged over the entire area. A soil test is only as good as the sample, so it is important to collect a representative sample of the site. Avoid unrepresentative areas where nutrient levels may be very high or very low.

A soil analysis has greater value if done in conjunction with a foliar analysis. In addition, there is still debate about the levels of various elements that are critical for tree growth. Thus, interpretation may be difficult. One way to facilitate interpretation is to compare foliar nutrient samples with samples from healthy trees of the same species. Leaf samples taken from symptomatic areas may help diagnose certain deficiencies or

Figure 4. When taking a soil sample, take six to ten cores from representative locations of the area.

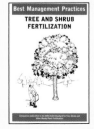

Table 2. Commonly available fertilizers, speed of availability, salt index, and soil reactions.

Product	Typical Nutrient Content %			Availability	Reaction (pH)	Salt Index*
	N	P₂O₅	K₂O			
Blood, dried	12	0	0	Medium	Slightly acidic	3
Bone meal	1–4	22–30	0	Slow	Alkaline	3.5
Cotton seed meal	8	2	2	Slow	Slightly acidic	3
Manure, Cow	1.5	1	1.5	Medium	Neutral	3.5
Manure, Poultry	2–3	1	1–2	Slow	Highly variable	**
Manure, Sheep	2–3	1	1–2	Slow		3.5
Municipal Sewage Sludge	2–5	1–4	0–0.5	Slow	Slightly acidic	1–3
Wood Ash, Hardwood	0	2	8	Slow	Alkaline	**
Ammonium Sulfate	21	0	0	Quick	Very acidic	69
Ammonium Nitrate	35	0	0	Quick	Acidic	105
Isobutylidene diurea (IBDU)	31	0	0	Slow	Acidic	6
Phosphate, Diammonium	18–21	46–53	0	Quick	Acidic	34
Phosphate, Monoammonium	12	61	0	Quick	Very acidic	25
Phosphate, Monopotassium	0	52	35	Quick	Acidic	8
Phosphate, Super	0	20	0	Slow	Neutral	8
Phosphate, Triple Super	0	48	0	Medium slow	Neutral	10
Potassium Chloride	0	0	60	Quick	Neutral	116
Potassium Nitrate	13	0	44–46	Quick	Alkaline	74
Potassium Sulfate	0	0	50–54	Medium	Neutral	46
Nitrate, Calcium	12	0	0	Quick	Alkaline	53
Nitrate, Sodium	16	0	0	Very quick	Alkaline	100
Ureaformaldehyde	38	0	0	Slow	Acidic	10
Urea	46	0	0	Quick	Acidic	75
Urea, Methylene	40	0	0	Medium	Acidic	27
Urea, Sulfur-Coated	22–38	0	0	Medium	Acidic	**

*To determine the salt index on a per unit of plant nutrient basis, divide the listed value by the sum of the percentage of N, P, and K.
**Information not available.

toxicities. However, a soil analysis or foliar analysis alone can be misleading. It is possible for certain minerals to be deficient in the leaves but plentiful in the soil and unavailable due to the soil pH level.

Current practices in the tree care industry are based on what is known as prescription fertilization—applying only nutrients that have been found to be deficient. This is an apt term, keeping in mind the medical saying, "prescription without diagnosis is malpractice."

Fertilizer Selection

Fertilizers are available in many forms and combinations (Figure 5). A complete fertilizer contains nitrogen, phosphorus, and potassium. The fertilizer analysis or guaranteed analysis listed on the container gives the composition of the fertilizer expressed as a percentage by weight of total nitrogen (N), available phosphoric acid (P₂O₅), and soluble potash (K₂O), always listed in the same order. For example, a fertilizer with an analysis of 9-3-3 contains 9 percent nitrogen, 3 percent phosphorus, and 3 percent potassium. A

50-pound bag of this fertilizer would contain 4.5 pounds of nitrogen. Fertilizer ratio can be determined by dividing each of the analysis numbers by the lowest number in the group. A 9-3-3 analysis therefore is a 3:1:1 ratio fertilizer.

Fertilizers are available in either organic or inorganic forms. Inorganic fertilizers release their elements relatively quickly when dissolved in water. The available nutrients are in the form of inorganic ions, which are adsorbed by oppositely charged sites on the root membrane. These same ions are also responsible for plant "burn" (when in excess concentration) by raising the osmotic pressure of soil solution and drawing water out of the roots.

Organic fertilizers also release inorganic ions but do so more slowly as the molecules are hydrolyzed or decomposed in the soil. Organic fertilizers are composed of carbon-based molecules and can be either synthetic or natural. Examples of synthetic organics are ureaformaldehyde (UF), methylene urea

Figure 5. Many fertilizer products are available. Recommendations for fertilization should be based on nutrient needs.

(MU), and isobutylidene diurea (IBDU). Examples of natural organics are manures, sewage sludge, blood, and bone meal. Urea, which contains a single carbon atom, is technically an organic. However, it is not recognized as such in the industry because of how rapidly it solubilizes and releases nitrogen ions in water.

Roots absorb most elements in the form of inorganic ions, whether coming from an organic or inorganic source. An advantage of organic fertilizers is that they must be converted to inorganic ions before absorption and, therefore, they are not leached as readily from the soil. One advantage of inorganic fertilizers is that solubility is less affected by temperature so that the rate of availability is more uniform.

Fertilizers with slow- or controlled-release nitrogen (CRN) should be used when fertilizing trees. This practice reduces the amount of fertilizer that may be leached and reduces salt or fertilizer "burn" problems. If slow-release fertilizer is used, more nitrogen can be applied at one time. To determine if a fertilizer is slow release, look for the percentage of water-insoluble nitrogen (WIN) on the label. If at least half of the nitrogen is water insoluble, the fertilizer is considered slow release.

The Other Macroelements: Sulfur, Phosphorus, and Postassium

Sulfur, phosphorus, and potassium occasionally are found lacking in trees and shrubs. When these elements are to be included in a fertilizer mix, there are many product options. Rates of application should be guided by soil and/or foliar nutrient analysis.

The Secondary Elements: Calcium and Magnesium

Calcium and magnesium deficiencies typically are found in acidic and sandy soils but may occur in any soil type. The common treatment for both deficiencies is application of dolomitic limestone. This fertilizer contains both elements. Rates of application are determined by soil and/or foliar nutrient analysis and by soil pH level. Because dolomitic limestone is used to increase soil pH,

when applying it for fertilization purposes, rates must not be so high that the soil pH is increased beyond the optimal range for the plant species.

Deficiency of calcium alone calls for the application of calcitic limestone on low pH soils or gypsum on high pH soils. Magnesium deficiency is treated with magnesium sulfate.

The Microelements: Iron, Manganese, Zinc, Boron, and Copper

Microelement deficiencies often are seen on high-pH (alkaline) soils, sandy soils, and/or soils with naturally low levels of these elements. These deficiencies are very host specific; they will affect one tree species, but an adjacent tree of a different species may not be affected at all.

Microelements can be applied to the soil or foliage, or they can be injected into the xylem. For soil application of iron and manganese, chelated forms are preferred because they are less likely to be chemically tied up in the soil. Salt forms of zinc, copper, and boron are often used. Application rates depend on the degree of deficiency, soil type, and product used.

Fertilizer pH

With regular application, most fertilizers will affect the pH of the soil (Table 2). In turn, soil pH affects the availability of many fertilizers. Therefore, when selecting a fertilizer, consider soil pH. General considerations are as follows:

- If pH is less than 5.0, use a nonammonical source of nitrogen
- If pH is above 7.2 or if the soil is too alkaline for the plant species, an acidifying fertilizer is preferred
- If pH is between 5.0 and 7.2, most other fertilizers can be used
- If soil pH is too acidic for the plant species, apply lime with the fertilizer or use an alkaline form of fertilizer

Salt Index

The salt index is a measure of the relative salinity of a fertilizer. Salts draw water out of the root system, resulting in less water uptake by the plant. Damage caused by the

salt is referred to as "salt burn" or "fertilizer burn." Fertilizers with high salt indices have a greater potential to cause desiccation of plants when applied at the same rate as fertilizers with low salt indices. For fertilizing trees and shrubs, a salt index of less than 50 is preferred to reduce the risk of plant damage.

Fertilizer Timing

Fertilizer uptake in deciduous hardwoods corresponds with the time of root growth. In general, root growth starts before budbreak and ends after leaf drop. The time of maximum nutrient uptake is from after budbreak in the spring to color change in the autumn. Avoid application of quick-release fertilizers between leaf drop and budbreak because uptake is minimal and fertilizer may be leached or volatilized.

In semitropical and Mediterranean climates, time of application is based on season of rainfall unless the plants are irrigated. Because nutrient uptake depends on water uptake, the fertilizer should be in place before or during the rainy season. In semitropical areas and areas with sandy soils and high rainfall or heavy irrigation, the frequency of applications may have to be increased.

With most slow-release fertilizers, the period of nutrient release is much longer. This fact makes the seasonal timing of application much less critical. Fall application of fertilizer does not normally predispose a plant to winter injury unless it is stressed by other factors (for example, shearing) or is grown outside its native range.

To prevent fertilizer runoff in the spring, avoid fertilizer application if the ground is frozen. During drought periods, roots will not readily absorb fertilizers. There also is the additional risk of damage from salts in the fertilizer; therefore, avoid application during droughts.

This article summarizes the advantages and limitations of tree fertilization, the considerations given to timing, and the types of fertilizer commonly used for trees. The second article in this series will deal with application techniques and calculating fertilizer amounts.

The ANSI A300 standard for fertilizing trees and shrubs was released in 1998. In addition, the International Society of Arboriculture has recently published *Best Management Practices: Tree and Shrub Fertilization*, which is intended to serve as a companion publication for the standard. Both publications are available through ISA.

Tom Smiley is an arboricultural researcher at the Bartlett Tree Research Laboratories and adjunct professor at Clemson University. Sharon Lilly is director of educational goods and services for ISA. Patrick Kelsey is a soil scientist at Christopher B. Burke Engineering and also is a Certified Professional Soil Scientist.

TEST QUESTIONS

To receive continuing education unit (CEU) credit (1 CEU) for home study of this article, after you have read it, darken the appropriate circles on the answer form in the back of this book. **Be sure to use the answer form that corresponds to this article.** Each question has only one correct answer. A passing score for this test is 80 percent. Photocopies of the answer form are **not** acceptable.

After you have answered the questions on the answer form, complete the registration information on the form and send it to ISA, P.O. Box 3129, Champaign, IL 61826-3129.

You will be notified only if you do not pass. CEU codes for the exams you have passed will appear on your CEU updates. If you do not pass, you have the option of taking the test as often as necessary.

1. Urban soils might not contain adequate levels of certain essential elements because
   a. topsoil may have been removed during construction
   b. leaves are raked and removed
   c. natural nutrient cycling is often interrupted
   d. all of the above

2. Trees might not require supplemental fertilization if they are
   a. in soil with a high pH
   b. located in or near heavily fertilized turf
   c. growing in sandy soils
   d. irrigated regularly

3. Nitrogen is critical to photosynthesis because it
   a. bonds with carbon molecules to form carbohydrates
   b. is the base molecule of all simple sugars
   c. splits the water molecule to provide hydrogen and oxygen
   d. is a constituent of the chlorophyll molecule

4. Positively charged ammonium ions are adsorbed to clay particles but
   a. only elemental nitrogen can be absorbed by the fine, fibrous plant roots
   b. ammonium ions cannot be converted to nitrate or nitrite ions
   c. negatively charged nitrate ions are free in the soil for uptake by plant roots or leaching
   d. all of the above

5. Not all of the nitrogen in the soil is taken up by plants because
   a. much is lost as a result of volatilization and leaching
   b. chelated forms of the molecules are chemically tied up
   c. nitrogen in the form of nitrate ions is unavailable
   d. all of the above

6. Symptoms of reduced growth, small leaves, and chlorosis of (primarily) the older leaves are typical of
   a. potassium deficiency
   b. phosphorus deficiency
   c. iron deficiency
   d. nitrogen deficiency

7. Although phosphorus and potassium are included in "complete" fertilizers, they usually aren't deficient in most landscape plants because
   a. adequate amounts usually are available in the soil
   b. plants can extract these minerals from the atmosphere
   c. most trees do not require phosphorus and potassium
   d. they are naturally synthesized as a byproduct of respiration

8. Which of the following element is commonly deficient in palms?
   a. magnesium
   b. copper
   c. potassium
   d. molybdenum

9. Symptoms such as small, chlorotic young leaves, often with green veins, and older leaves of darker green are typical of a deficiency of
   a. nitrogen
   b. iron
   c. sulfur
   d. potassium

10. Fertilizer may not be necessary or beneficial when trees or shrubs have
    a. sufficient levels of essential elements
    b. potential for certain pest problems
    c. herbicide damage with residual activity in the plant
    d. all of the above

11. A limitation of using foliar nutrient analysis in making recommendations is that
    a. there is no test for micronutrient levels
    b. it does not provide information about why nutrients are deficient
    c. it measures only the nutrients that have been absorbed recently
    d. results don't correlate well with nutrients that are actually present in the leaves

12. A soil analysis usually will provide information about
    a. the presence of certain nutrients
    b. soil pH and CEC
    c. organic matter content
    d. all of the above

13. Which of the following mineral elements is most commonly limiting in landscape plants?
    a. iron
    b. phosphorus
    c. nitrogen
    d. potassium

14. Nitrogen levels are difficult to measure in soil analysis because
    a. only the elemental gas form of nitrogen is measurable using laboratory techniques
    b. nitrogen is present in such minute quantities
    c. it leaches readily from the soil
    d. nitrogen exists in numerous forms in the soil and transforms between them

15. High levels of organic matter usually correlate with
    a. high levels of available nutrients
    b. coarse-textured soils
    c. extremely high soil pH measurements
    d. all of the above

16. A 25-pound bag of fertilizer with an analysis of 10-3-4 (approximate ratio of 3:1:1) would contain how many pounds of actual nitrogen?
    a. 1
    b. 2.5
    c. 3
    d. 4

17. An advantage of using slow-release fertilizers is that
    a. salt or fertilizer "burn" usually is less of a problem
    b. they are not leached as readily as quick-release fertilizers
    c. applications need not be as frequent
    d. all of the above

18. A nonammonical source of nitrogen is recommended when the pH is
    a. less than 5.0
    b. between 5.0 and 7.2
    c. between 7.2 and 8.0
    d. greater than 8.0

19. To reduce the risk of plant damage when fertilizing trees and shrubs, look for a salt index of
    a. less than 50
    b. 50 to 75
    c. 75 to 100
    d. no less than 100

20. Maximum nutrient uptake usually occurs
    a. before budbreak in the spring
    b. between budbreak and color change in the autumn
    c. just after leaf fall in the autumn
    d. during the winter dormant months

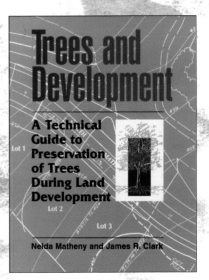

FERTILIZING TREES AND SHRUBS

PART 2 Application Techniques

By E. Thomas Smiley, Sharon Lilly, and Patrick Kelsey

Part 1 of this article dealt with trees' essential element requirements, soil and foliar testing, when fertilizer may or may not be indicated, pH interactions, and the various types of fertilizers. This article picks up with application techniques and contrasts the advantages and limitations of the various techniques commonly in use.

Fertilizer Application

Fertilizers can be applied to the soil or foliage, or they can be injected directly into the xylem of trees. Soil application is the preferred technique. Foliar spray or trunk injections should be reserved for rare cases when soil application is not effective or not practical to apply.

Soil surface application of fertilizer is an efficient means of delivering nitrogen to trees or shrubs. Nitrogen is very mobile in the soil, so as long as there is an adequate amount of water moving through the soil, the nitrogen will move to the root area. Dry surface applications are made with carried or wheeled fertilizer spreaders. These types

> **Learning objectives—**
> **The arborist will be able to**
> - contrast the various application techniques for fertilizing trees and discuss the advantages and limitations of each.
> - calculate fertilization application areas.
> - calculate fertilizer amounts.
> - discuss techniques for calibrating applicators.

of spreaders provide an even distribution of the material if moved at a constant speed. To avoid loss of fertilizer efficacy, applications should be made immediately before rain or irrigation, whenever possible.

Liquid surface application can be made with a variety of spray equipment. To achieve an even distribution of the fertilizer, a flooding tip or water breaker nozzle is preferred for surface application.

Although surface application can be effective and inexpensive, there are some use limitations. Where the fertilizer application area is covered with turf, the turf takes up a portion of surface fertilizer. Surface-applying fertilizer on organic mulch increases the breakdown rate of the mulch because of an increase in biological activity. On slopes, surface-applied fertilizers

Surface application can be effective and inexpensive, but it does have some limitations.

are more likely to run off. Phosphorus may not move into the root area of trees before it is tied up in the soil. In this case, a subsurface application of fertilizer is preferred. Potassium is intermediate in soil mobility; subsurface application is the preferred application technique, but surface application may be effective in many cases.

Subsurface, drill-hole application of fertilizer requires drilling holes to a depth of 4 to 12 inches (4 to 8 inches, preferably) and pouring a specified amount of fertilizer into each hole. There should be at least 2 inches between the top of the fertilizer and the surface of the soil. The same amount of fertilizer should be applied to each hole.

Hole diameter should be 2 to 4 inches. The most common size of earth auger used for this purpose is 2 inches in diameter. Hole spacing should be 12 to 36 inches. The closer spacing should be used when additional soil aeration is desired, such as in a compacted soil. When more holes are

Soil surface application is an efficient means of delivering nitrogen.

drilled, less fertilizer is applied to each hole. All holes should be evenly spaced within the fertilization application area; usually a grid pattern is used.

Subsurface, liquid injection is the most common application method used by commercial arborists. When applying fertilizer with this technique, injection sites should be evenly spaced within the fertilization area to a depth of 4 to 12 inches. In most cases, injection at depths less than 4 inches will result in fertilizer bubbling to the soil surface. Injection to depths greater than 8 inches will result in fertilizer being delivered deeper than the fine roots of most trees. Fertilizer placed below the actively absorbing roots is likely to leach away. Therefore, the preferred depth of application is 4 to 8 inches.

The quantity of liquid injected into each hole typically is 1 to 2 quarts. Higher rates often lead to unintentional surface application when the solution bubbles to the soil surface. At these rates, using a pressure of 150 to 200 psi (measured at the pump), the typical distribution radius is 18 inches, which provides good coverage when using 36-inch spacing.

Fertilizer Application Area

The area in which fertilizer is applied should correspond to the maximum concentration of fine, absorbing roots in the soil. Generally, these roots are in the upper 6 inches of soil. On open-grown trees, fine roots are found from near the trunk to well beyond the drip line of the tree. Beyond the drip line, however, root concentration drops off at a relatively high rate. Therefore, fertilizer application should be made from near the trunk to near the drip line.

If soil injecting or using drill-hole techniques, avoid damage to the buttress roots of the tree when working near the trunk. Avoid the areas immediately outside the point where buttress roots enter the soil. Instead, apply between the buttress roots or root flares.

On trees with a dense canopy, such as Norway maple (*Acer platanoides*) and pin

Subsurface, liquid injection is the most common application method.

oak (*Quercus palustris*), fine-root density often is higher at the drip line than immediately inside it, possibly because of the water runoff pattern. On trees with this characteristic, application beyond the drip line may be beneficial.

Pine (*Pinus* spp.) and other coniferous trees tend to have a less wide-spreading root system than hardwoods. On such species, it is not necessary to fertilize all the way to the drip line.

When fertilizing a group of trees or small woodlot, the entire area within the drip line of the group should be treated. It is not necessary or desirable to calculate the fertilizer area for each tree and add them up. Instead, calculate the area for the entire group.

If there is pavement such as sidewalks or streets, or if there is a structure within the drip line of the tree, this area should be subtracted from the fertilizer application area. Compensating for these impermeable surfaces by adding additional fertilizer in other areas is not necessary.

When fertilizing fastigiate (narrow) trees, trees with small canopies, or trees that were pruned to an unusual shape, the drip line is not a good guide to the area of maximum fine-root concentration. In these cases, a fertilizer application area can be calculated from the trunk diameter. Multiply the diameter measured in inches at 4.5 feet (dbh) by either 1 or 1.5 to get a number,

expressed in feet, to use as the radius measurement for the fertilization area. For example, a 15-inch dbh tree would have a fertilization area of 15 to 23 feet in radius, depending on the multiplication factor selected.

When writing a contract for fertilization, you must specify the fertilizer area. This can be done by stating that fertilizer should be applied from near the trunk to the drip line, or it can be specified as a distance such as from the trunk to a radius of 10 feet.

Fertilizer Application Area Calculations

One of the most important aspects of determining fertilizer rates is correctly calculating the area where fertilizer will be applied. To make this calculation, you must measure the area. This measurement usually is done by visualizing the area as either a circle or a rectangle. When determining the fertilization area of an open-grown tree, the area is visualized as a circle with the trunk at the center. The area (A) of a circle is equal to the radius (r) multiplied by itself then multiplied by 3.14 ($A = 3.14 \times r \times r$). A tree with a drip-line radius of 10 feet will have an area of about 314 square feet to fertilize ($3.14 \times 10 \times 10 = 314$).

The second method of calculating area is by visualizing a rectangle. To calculate the area of a rectangle, multiply the length by the width.

Fertilizer Rates

The rate of fertilizer to apply should be determined by the landscape goals and the current nutrient status of the soil. Whenever possible, the results of soil analysis, foliar analysis, or both should be used to provide information on nutrient status. Without guidance of nutrient analysis, the following guidelines can be used.

The standard rates for slow-release fertilizer are 2 to 4 pounds nitrogen per 1,000 square feet, not to exceed 6 pounds of nitrogen per 1,000 square feet annually. Higher rates may lead to a greater potential